TESTIMONIALS FOR
TONI LUISA RIVERA, DC

When I first saw Dr. Toni Luisa Rivera as a patient several years ago, I knew she had a very different approach when she asked me about a 25 year-old ankle injury that I hadn't reported to her in my medical history. Since that time, my inner experience of my life, as well as my physical well-being, have been enhanced by Toni's intuitive guidance. In this book, Dr. Toni shares her insights and skills. ~MLU

When working with Dr. Toni as a client and student I experience a subtle yet powerful change in my way of viewing things by trusting my intuition and following the guidance that I asked for. Now there is flow flow flow. The sadness and anger is gone and I feel renewed with enthusiasm and the joy of living. Sensing energy and the power and intelligence of the body/mind connection excites me. The theme of curiosity has a joyful quality. ~N.A.

Dr. Toni Luisa Rivera is an intelligent, attentive, compassionate, skilled healer. My sessions with Toni are filled with the grace of her open and generous heart; I feel the healing energy flowing from her hands to exactly where it needs to go. She can locate and relieve the physical symptom(s) I have presented to her. I am safe with Toni and trust her implicitly. ~N.B.

I have been Dr. Toni's patient since 2002. I experienced a stroke in 2001 and had residual problems that continued to cause me issues. I was referred to Dr. Toni and have continued to see her at least every three weeks since that time and I can't imagine my treatment plan without her. When I had a procedure to close a hole in my heart in 2003, she helped me face that process both emotionally and physically. When the hole didn't close in the "normal" amount of time, she helped me to understand the intricacies of my body & spirit so that I could maintain hope. There have been so many times that she has decreased the nerve pain I feel, as well as to help me understand it from an emotional and spiritual level. She has been there for me during the ups and downs of life as well as providing guidance as I handle my disability. She has taught me many "things" about caring for myself, listening to my body's messages, trusting my own intuition about my needs, acceptance of my disability, and much more. Although I will continue to deal with chronic issues, because of her teachings, I can now intervene on several levels to help myself maintain a life that allows me to participate as fully as possible. I could continue to cite many examples of the benefits I have received from Dr. Toni however I will make one final statement. I don't know what direction my life would have taken if I hadn't received the critical care needed to help me recover from my stroke and to help me maintain the quality of life I now have. I owe so much to her. ~S.M. August 4, 2015

Dr. Toni Luisa Rivera is the proverbial "Miracle Worker." She cured a 30-year backache, and she completely restores my body ongoing. ~R.P.

Having carved hard rock for 16 years I have needed the care of Dr. Toni Luisa Rivera for about 10 years now; probably more, if not for my stubbornness and youth of that time. Her alternative approach to care has been eye opening. She has enabled me to see the connectedness of not just my actions, but of my body and my self. The fascial sheaths, the inner physical self, and the energy that *is* us. That physical ailments can manifest due to our emotional and spiritual actions. She is my primary doctor, but is also an important voice and friend in my life. ~J.G.

After moving to Santa Fe, I called to schedule a treatment for my wife with Dr. Toni because she was referred to us. There was a 6 month waiting period for new patients. It is now 15 years later. Kathryn and I are still relying on her extraordinary sensitivity, vision and total understanding of her profession. We love her and trust her talents for our physical, mental and emotional well being. It is understandable that there is a waiting list to see her. She is absolutely amazing!" ~R.D.

I have been a patient of Dr. Toni Rivera for 20 years. I am a dental hygienist and have been practicing full time for 28 years. Considering the body positions and repetitive motions hygienists experience on a daily basis, I naturally needed help to be able to continue practicing. I have seen other chiropractors - usually on an emergency basis. The difference is striking. Dr. Rivera listens to my body and adjusts me accordingly. Rarely has she needed to do a structural adjustment. In fact, several times in the past I have asked her to just because "I" felt I really needed it. She would reply - "your body doesn't agree." Later after the appointment, I would realize, she was right because the issue had resolved without being "cracked" or some other forceful adjustment. Bottom line - Dr. Rivera is simply amazing and I can honestly say I would not still be practicing dental hygiene if not for her! She truly knows the intricate aspects of how all the body's parts interact including the body/mind connection, not just the skeletal aspects. ~C.S.

"I have been a patient of Dr. Toni Rivera's for over 15 years. Toni's work has profoundly improved my life. Her integrity, intuition, immense understanding and knowledge of the human body, mind, and spirit, have created a very safe place from which I feel a true sense of evolving. She inspires joy and truth, and I would have no hesitation in saying that she is one of the most gifted healers I have ever met." ~K.D.

"I've been skateboarding at a semi-professional level for the past 8 years. Toni is the reason why I am still skateboarding to this day. If it had not been for her, I would have stopped doing the sport I love years ago.

Toni has a vast wealth of knowledge when it comes to the body, intuition and how to truly coach people on furthering their own intuitive abilities. Every lesson is filled with multiple 'light-bulb moments' when we meet." ~ L.S.

The Propelled Heart

The
Propelled
HEART

Moving from
Injury to Insight

Toni Luisa Rivera, DC

PROPELLED HEART
PUBLISHING

Santa Fe, New Mexico

This book is dedicated to my loving parents.

They helped me become who I am today.

Thank you from the depths of my heart.

ACKNOWLEDGEMENTS

I want to thank all the souls who have touched my life. Without the experiences we have shared, the richness of my life could not have been achieved. There are too many of you to name here – please know that there is love within me for each of you.

Deep thanks to my primary life mentors. My mother was the first, from inception. I would not fully understand her depth of feeling, and deep faith, until she had left this earth. One of her favorite sayings, which drove me crazy as a teen – "It will all work out" – was actually a testament to her strong will and commitment to family and God.

My father, my spiritual family from other life times. With his warmth, love, strength and humor, he guides me to this day with his love of life, beaming good will and spiritual fortitude. "You can be and do whatever you put your mind to!" he said. "I believe in you and am here to support you always!"

My mentors and teachers: Dr. Larry J. Troxell, without whom I would not have been able to start and sustain my first chiropractic practice. He shared his wisdom and expertise willingly. He guided me to know the physical body, and how to facilitate healing of the spine and nervous system through the chiropractic physical adjustment. "Serve the people," he said, "they need you and no one else can help them the way you can through chiropractic."

Ilana Rubenfeld, who opened my heart and mind to the richness of life. The life within me and all of humankind. She brought music and art into my life. She taught me how to teach others through creating an experience for them, allowing each one to discover their own insights. "Listen with your whole being," she said, "the body always tells the truth."

Joe Weldon, who helped me see my own wounds, with his way of Being and his words. He showed me how I subconsciously used these wounds to create the avenues by which I might feed the needs of my inner child. "Notice how you get people to feel the way they do about you." he said. "I wish you could realize that you don't *owe* anyone anything."

Noel Wight, who showed me how to be a strong woman, and to love myself just as I am. She embodies integrity, strength of character and love. "You are good and worthy just as you are, Toni," she said. "I love you. You don't have to take care of me to be worthy of that love."

My beloved Rubenfeld Synergy Teaching Intern friends, whose respect and love sustain me to this day: Tanzy Maxfield, Dawn Garcia, Donna Marie Berry and Gay Marcontell. Our pre-training check-ins were life enriching, and they taught me what it means to be a friend and to receive friendship.

So many more to thank. The friends of my youth from Puerto Rico, who to this day, when we meet, it seems like only a few days have passed as we fall right back into sync. You have helped me be me! Many blessings to you all!

From Santa Fe: My brothers and sisters on the spiritual path in the Santa Fe Meditation Circle, Jai Guru! We have been together before, and we are gathered here for that one purpose. "Everything else can wait, but your search for God cannot wait." Paramahansa Yogananda.

Dan Pauli, music teacher and friend, and all my marimba sisters and brothers. May we long play the music of our African ancestors. "Groove or Die" is the cry of the rhythm.

I must mention the *Leader to Luminary* team from Vancouver, B.C.: Callan Rush, Josh Decker, Kate Irwin, Sheena Marie, and all the rest of those wonderful people. They helped me face some deep issues that were holding me back from my full expression as a workshop leader. Actually, my full expression as an authentic person walking this earth.

My most recent mentors for this new phase of my life: my thanks to you!

Author It! Co-leaders, Candace Walsh and Tanya Rubinstein.

Tom Bird, my most recent and important mentor and role model for writing, leading, and being all I can be! "Write from God," he said. And then he showed me how! "Write your dream and then live into it!" and then he showed me how. Thank you!

Many thanks to all my patients and clients over the years. For your trust in me. For allowing me to be a part of your healing journey. It is an honor!

NAMASTE!

CONTENTS

INTRODUCTION

The quest for deeper knowledge, and an understanding of the meaning of life, is the journey of the propelled heart. The experiences of life may bring injury to the physical, mental or emotional aspects of an individual. The propelled heart has the attitude of wanting to move forward in life. To learn about how the relationships, experiences and various interactions can serve as opportunities for the evolution of Being. I invite you to join me on this quest.

Part I of this book chronicles my story of moving from injury to insight into how the wounds have transformed into gifts for the world around me. Part II imparts ways to tap into the wisdom within you, and includes exercises which will allow insight into your own life.

Go online to *ToniLuisaRivera.com* for MP3 downloads of the exercises.

PREFACE

In the past, fear plagued my sleep time. I would wake with a start and have a deep ache in my chest, and be unable to catch my breath. Details would escape me. "What is going on!" I would question myself, to no avail. Sometimes the fear would seem to be from something going on in my life at the time. Money, love or something I had said or done, or something coming up soon. As the years wore on, it became apparent that there was some hidden cause. It didn't matter what was going on in the now. There was something from the past that had brought fear into my life, into my very cells. Something that was now hidden. Something I couldn't quite touch. I would have glimpses in some therapy session or in a dream. Then, it became apparent that I had to face the fear itself. The fear that had been embedded within my psyche, and now needed only a minor trigger to set it off in my sleep.

There was a sailing trip once. We sailed fourteen-foot Hobie Cats from Puerto Rico to the end of the British Virgin Islands. A Hobie Cat is a small catamaran (a boat with two hulls), the brain child of Hobart "Hobie" Alter. It's a fun, easy-to-sail boat that won't go slow. If there is wind, you are moving. If you sail well, you can "fly a hull," lifting one pontoon out of the water and zooming on the other across the sea. There were five of us on three boats. My friend from high school, Barb, and a friend of hers from freshman year at college were on one Hobie; Barb's parents on another one; and me, solo, on another. I was eighteen and an average sailor. Hobie Cat hulls (or pontoons) are fiberglass. They have a square aluminum frame between the pontoons. A strong plastic mesh material for a deck, called a trampoline, stretches across the frame between the pontoons. The fourteen-foot Hobie Cat has only one sail. The mast is hoisted while on the beach by two people. One person stands on the material deck, allowing the mast to slide through their hands, and pushing it upright as it moves toward them. The other person, standing on the beach, moves quickly towards the boat, pushing the bottom end of the mast toward the ground and then lifting it straight up at the last minute, placing it into the metal cup on the frame. This cup is designed to allow the mast to swivel according to the sail's position. The mast is then attached to its forestay and shrouds (the wires that hold it up). We sailed by sight. There was no such thing as "relaxing on deck," unless there was absolutely no wind.

We sailed away from Fajardo, Puerto Rico, on the far eastern shore, in the late afternoon that summer. We had driven, with the boats on trailers, from our homes on the northwestern shore of the island. As we sailed away, my parents got smaller and smaller, waving from the shoreline. I had no idea of the adventure that awaited us. We sailed to Culebrita, a small island just off Puerto Rico, to stay the night. It was the last land before our passage to St. Thomas the next day. We could barely make out St. Thomas in the distance, from the lighthouse on Culebrita, as the sun set. Excitement stirred in my belly.

We made camp for the night, as we would every night of our two-week trip. During our sail, we carried our gear in waterproof bags strapped to the trampoline near the mast. We would pull up on a beach every evening, make camp and cook out on a fire we made from driftwood. We slept on the decks of our Hobies, stars overhead. If there was rain we used the sail as a makeshift tent, rigging it to hang over the boom and then the sides of the frame. Early in the morning we arose and cooked breakfast and repacked the gear, establishing our daily ritual. That first day was sunny and clear. The sea was fairly calm, with a good wind starting.

We pushed off from the shore and jumped onto the trampolines of the little boats, the sails filling with wind immediately, and we scooted off to sea. As we sailed away from the beach that day, there were no waving family members. Just the palm trees, waving their fronds in the breeze.

There had been no mention of how long the passage would take to St. Thomas, and I had not thought to ask. St. Thomas is the first of the Lesser Antilles, the closest U.S. Virgin Island to Puerto Rico. The time of the crossing and its harshness or ease would depend on the wind and the strong current that governed the passage between the two islands. The tiny island with the lighthouse, where we had spent the night, had now receded and was no longer visible. Occasional glimpses of a shadow that was St. Thomas peeped at us between the swells. I was confident and happy to be on this adventure.

Barb was the most talented sailor. Always the confident, brave one, she set a tack that was her own, and disappeared quickly into the distance ahead. She had a way of finding the tack that took the most advantage of the wind and squeezed the most speed out of it. I maneuvered my boat to stay close to her parents. I didn't want to go it completely alone! As we approached the middle of the passage, the swells grew. They were now so tall that even though I was close enough to yell to her parents, the top of their twenty-five-foot mast disappeared from view when my boat was in a trough between waves. They encouraged me to "fall off" so as not to block their wind. No way! I was staying as close as possible without blocking their wind! As we sailed along that day, I felt very alone and completely self reliant, as it seems I have been all my life. More on that later. I was alone with myself and my thoughts as the hours slipped away. The occasional glimpses of St. Thomas, when I was positioned on top of one of the swells, were few and far between. It was open sea. The splashing of the water on the hulls as I cut through the swells, the "tick-tick" of the forestay on the mast, and the blowing of the wind were my only companions. We were moving quite quickly, and I had to "hike out" to keep the boat from capsizing. "Hiking out" is when you sit on the very edge of the frame of the deck, your feet under straps sewn to the trampoline so you don't slip off, legs extended fully, and leaning backwards out over the water to counterbalance the force of the wind in the sail. It had been hours, four at least, and I was getting tired. Images of possible disasters started to flood my mind. "What if a whale comes up under the boat!" I imagined, seeing myself on my little orange boat with the yellow sail lifted out of the water on the back of the huge beast. "Well, I'll just have to see what happens!" "What if the wind changes suddenly and the sail jibes around the other side of the boat and throws me off!" "What if I put my arm up to stop the sail from jibing and the boom breaks my arm!" What if, what if, what if went on for a long while. I'd finally had enough of these awful thoughts. "Okay, Toni! You're either going to live or die! Stop it right now! Stop thinking those awful things and just sail the boat! We are going to make it! And if something happens, you will just have to deal with it!" I sailed onward. "Refocus on the positive, and do what you can do right now!"

More time passed; I didn't know how much. My little personal pep talk had rallied me, and I calmed down and focused on optimizing the little boat's performance. On enjoying the little riffs on the swells, the sights of birds soaring overhead, and the schools of flying fish, launching themselves up and over the water as I rushed by.

Finally, we were close enough to St. Thomas to see the rocky western edge of the shore. We kept sailing. It seemed as though we weren't moving at all. "This is the worst of the current. That's why we are barely moving forward, though the wind is blowing like hell! Just keep your course!" Bruz, Barb's dad, had come close and yelled to me. "Can't we just pull up here?" I pleaded. It had been over seven hours, and I was exhausted. My belly ached from hiking out and my arms and legs were starting to spasm. "No! There is a reef here, and we can't go up on the rocks! We have to get around the northwest point and pass Charlotte Amalie (the capital and main port of St. Thomas). Then we'll beach on the sandy shores near the Hilton after the port." I was in agony. "How much longer?" I yelled out over the wind. "Two or three hours!" was the reply. I was beginning to doubt if I'd make it! But what choice was there?

Up ahead, we saw that Barb's boat didn't have a mast up. She was floating, holding the mast on the deck. The forestay, holding the mast in place, had broken! Bruz was able to swim to her boat with supplies. They replaced the forestay, and righted the mast from the water! This was considered impossible in the manual! Yet, Bruz and Barb were strong and ingenious enough to pull it off. Ann, Barb's mom, and I were waiting nearby, with our two boats pointing into the wind so we could stay as stationary as possible. Bobbing on the surface of the sea, their rudders and sails complaining, the Hobies seemed to beg to get moving again. The current was pulling us back toward that reef and the rocky shore. After the agonizing wait, watching from afar, Bruz finally swam back to join Ann on their boat – and we were on our way again! I could taste the reward of one of those twenty-ounce, ice-cold Heinekens that awaited us at the hotel! It's one of the advantages of camping close to one of the luxury hotels or five-star resorts along the way. But that's another story. (Or many!)

We did finally make it to the sandy beach past the port of Charlotte Amalie. It had taken us over ten hours to make the passage. I've never been so tired in my life. And satisfied. Satisfied with myself for making it. Proud, really, that I had been able to face my fears and sail the boat alone. Ann complimented me on a job well done as the others started making camp. I was starving!

Little did I know at the time, but this sailing trip was a fitting metaphor for my life. This is the journey each of us makes in life. We must captain our ship, our life, facing the fears and challenges as they present themselves. Enjoying the sights and experiences as they come. The choice is ours. The boat has left the tiny island, and the journey to our next phase of life has begun. You can experience the victory of calm mind over fear. You can choose to rise to the challenge. You can heal body, mind, emotions and spirit.

This is the strength I call on now as I prepare to share this story of my life with you.

PART I

Injury
to Impasse

CHAPTER 1

The Closet

"If you're feeling contempt,
well then tell it...."
— JONI MITCHELL

The floor was hard and there was no air moving. I was tucked amid the shoes, my head not reaching up to the clothes which were above my head. The clothes were stuffed tightly together as the rack was so full. I sat with my knees bent up to my chest. Hugging my legs fiercely, with my forehead on my knees. I fought back the tears and cries. My throat felt as though one of those huge old cold metal ice tongs was pinching tightly as I squeezed my vocal cords to keep them quiet. My body ached. From low back to neck. Especially the neck. My heart ached, my throat stung. I was there a long time, rocking, rocking, rocking. Making solemn promises to my self – electrified with the high emotional charge – that would make them last a lifetime. These would be the guiding directions that my ego would unfold by, stretching over the next decades. "I am going to be grown up right now!" I repeated it again and again. "I am never going to let anyone know how much I hurt!" The serious vows made grooves in my brain. "I will never cry again," as I squeezed and squeezed my throat into submission. "I don't need anybody!" "I can do everything alone!" I chanted the vows again and again. Over and over. They had a rhythm now. Over and over as I rocked and hurt and squeezed the tears and cries out of my voice. "Never again! Never again!" I don't need anybody!" "I will never let them see how much they hurt me!" "Never, never, never!" Over and over, again and again, the words cemented the ideas into my psyche.

I was around four years old. My abuser had finally "gone all the way," and it had pushed me over the edge. I could no longer keep "our secret," and I had told my mom. She had become hysterical. Screaming, moaning and crying. "What is happening?" I thought. "This is so scary! What is wrong with her? What did I do to her? She is hurt. I hurt her. I have been so bad. Look at her. Feel her fear and cries! What have I done now?" I ran into the closet, her closet, and squeezed and squeezed. I should never have said anything. "Now I'm in trouble. What did I do? Why did I say anything. I am so bad! She is so upset now. I have been so bad. She hates me now. Why did I say anything? He told me not to say anything to anyone! What am I going to do now? How can I stop this? How can I go back. How can I undo the telling. Now she knows. How can I hide? Will this ever be over? I made a big mistake. She is not going to help me. She hates me now. I can still hear her crying. When will this be over? I hate myself. She hates me. Why did I tell the secret?"

The Closet has tentacles throughout my life, like a starfish, or a neuron. Reaching, reaching, far and wide. Once, after a very intense breath-work session, I went home to meditate. I had remembered The Closet, and I needed to sit with what was occurring within me. After a brief meditation, I was drawn to sit on the floor, the way I had been in The Closet. Back up against the wall. Legs bent up to my chest. Hugging my knees close, head bent, with my forehead on my knees. As I sat there, I began to feel tears welling up, rocking myself side to side slightly. The feelings were enormous. So much bigger than my body! I fought to contain them. Squeezing my knees close, squeezing my throat. Crushing it! I felt those old-time metal ice tongs, the pinching ends, boring holes into my throat. DON'T YOU DARE CRY! The pain in my throat reminded me of the thyroid disease I had been suffering with in the most recent years. The pain in my neck was the same pain as all the whiplash injuries. The headache, reminiscent of the feeling after the many concussions I suffered in high school horseback-riding accidents. The low-back pain, the familiar hip pain, the knee pain from sprains. The right leg and right arm pains like those of my worst horse accident. How could this be? All the pains, all the injuries, even the thyroid disease were here in this moment, in this position, right now! All of these painful incidents that were spread over my life. Every physical injury I had ever sustained, and the most dangerous disease I had suffered, had all had their seeds planted in my being, in my body, in that closet! Had those intense emotions cemented themselves into my very cells, preceding and producing all the injuries and sicknesses I had ever experienced?!

My father was in the Air Force at that time, and shortly after that we moved. The memory of the abuse faded from my little girl mind. Research has shown that memories from before the brain's growth spurt at around five years of age are stored in the cells of the body, not in the way memories are stored after that age. Not the way we store memories as adults, with words to describe events and a timeline to organize them. This is why many people are not sure if the bits and pieces they get flashes of are really true. Did those awful things really happen? This is how "false memory" syndrome can seem more of a reality than the possibility that something horrible happened to someone at a young age.

My first memory of abuse came one morning on awakening – at that time of morning when one is kind of awake but still in an altered state between waking and sleep. I felt like I had little girl legs. Little girl's legs instead of my adult legs! Now this was most peculiar! My legs felt short and very small and bare. Like a little girl! They looked, in my mind's eye, like little girl legs and they felt like little girl legs. So small, so strange!

It just so happened that I was to receive a Rubenfeld Synergy session that day. When I told the practitioner about waking up with the "little girl legs," she suggested that we explore that image and sensation. As I lay on the table and started going into my body, they reappeared. I felt the strange sensation of my legs being small, bare and very short. As I focused on them, I was transported back to some time long ago. Now I was a little girl lying flat on my back. I was very still, barely breathing. There was someone between my legs. There was a man and a woman. They were doing things to me which I could not see or feel. I couldn't feel anything anymore. It was as if I was seeing someone else. That these things were happening to someone else, not me. Yet, it was me there, lying on the table. I was supposed to be still so they could do whatever it was they were doing. I couldn't see their faces no matter how I tried. Who were they? What were they doing to me?

After many Rubenfeld Synergy sessions, exploring my body memories through touch and talk, we were led to my remembering other bits and pieces. I remembered years of my heart's energy being sucked out, until it bled energy. It had bled energy and cried, many times. Those little girl legs eventually led me to remembering the episode that led up to The Closet. When, in the secluded rocks, hidden from view, he had taken the last piece – that forbidden fruit. He hurt me so badly! He stuck the knife in and twisted it. He was an animal feasting on what was left of my innocence. He kneeled on my wrist and pulled my arm, contorting me so much, I could hardly breathe. My arm! My insides burned! I stopped fighting. He has killed me! Yet I live on!

My heart needs to live now. To live without worry. Without crying. Without thrashing. The tears that are stored in my heart need to be freed. The numbness in my arm that comes from my neck and shoulder. The first injury, the primary injury. What is happening there? My shoulder is chronically misaligned and disengaged. What does it have to disengage from? Life itself? This had been my modus operandi for years. Ever since The Closet. Disengaged from the pain, the hurt, the loneliness. The pain was great. The loneliness a wide river. No – an ocean of separation. No one saw me. No one heard my cries at night. No one saw the fear I was living in. My neck hurts right now as the memory comes. Where were my people? I was alone in the dark there. How alone I was. I had vowed to never let anyone close again. I have kept that promise as well as possible. After The Closet, I was strong. I was grown up. I didn't cry anymore. That was weakness. This is the reason for this book. To counter this. To deny those promises.

Years later, when first remembering The Closet, before remembering what had transpired there, I saw that there was a piece of wood at the back that didn't match the wall, nor lie flush with it. My first attempt to ask my parents what had happened met with some resistance. I only remembered The Closet's look, and not why I was there. They thought I must be having some confused memory. Something my mind had constructed. I recounted my memory of their room, what furniture was there, and how it was situated in the room. Then The Closet. That piece of wood that wasn't flush on the back wall. "How could you remember that?" Mom asked, confused. "There was to be an addition put on. That was the entrance to what would be the master bathroom. How could you know that? You were only around four years old!" The impression of the place where the intense emotions had occurred was imprinted on my memory.

The intensity of the memory had several causes. First, the culmination of the abuse and then my last hope for help, my mom. She didn't respond in a way that helped me. She was so shocked when I had told her that she left me alone with the tragedy. Left with the impression that I had been bad and done wrong. She did not ever talk with me about it. She never told me it wasn't my fault. I was left alone in The Closet, in my life, to deal with all the emotion, all the pain, all the hurt on my own. My little girl brain, trying to deal as best as possible with it all. That little girl made decisions based on what life experience she had in the moment. The promises were made to myself, forever etched in my brain. The effect of this experience with my mother overshadowed the injury of the abuse for me. Trust in others being willing, or able, to help me was shattered. The actual abuse also left scars on my ways of connecting with others, and on my ability to have healthy, close relationships. The benefits have been that I am very self-confident and self-reliant. Always able to make my way in the world. Triumph over tragedy? In some ways, yes. In some ways, no.

CHAPTER 2

Connection

*"...The human connection is the key
to personal and career success."*
— PAUL J. MEYER

Reflecting on connection. Connection with self, connection with others, connection with spirit, connection with life. What did I learn from my family about connecting? Mom had a hard time connecting with me as a baby: I had colic and cried a lot. She would get frustrated with me and leave me in the crib. Dad would connect with me when he came home by holding me on his chest until I fell asleep. Dad and I have always been very close. I am sure those times when he held me close to his heart for hours created this close bond that we now share.

Mom connected through food. She would make us all our meals. Delicious foods! From the breakfast, lunch and dinner, to scrumptious desserts. Lots of desserts! Cakes and pies and cookies. Ice cream and chocolate syrup. Yummy! "Are you hurting, little girl? Have a cookie or some ice cream," she comforted.

We had meat and potatoes and creamy gravy. It was good! That is how she served us. That is how she showed her love. That is how she connected with us. That is how love moved in her body, mind and spirit. She couldn't talk much about love. She couldn't remember her childhood. I always wondered why. Was there something she had blocked out? That she wanted or needed to forget?

Dad was very busy. He worked and thrived. He was challenged and received his kudos from his work. He also was always going to night school. He loved to learn. Both at work and at school. He had mom at home. The house was warm and the pots were full. The children were fed, clothed and awaiting his return. We loved him. He taught me to read at a very young age, before kindergarten. This is where my love of horses began. I read every book about horses they had in the library! He held me on his lap to read after those wonderful visits to the library. He hugged me a lot. He was the heart of our home. I missed him so much when he was not there.

Dad went to school "bootstrap" once. He was stationed at Shaw Air Force Base and arranged to go to Puerto Rico for school, preparing for when he would soon retire from the Air Force. He was gone for six months. I was distraught! I can remember the pain of coming home from school once, upset about something. Mom was watching her soap opera. She didn't even notice that I was so upset. I went to my room and cried alone.

I used to go to the Central Base Funds stable on base when we lived there in South Carolina. Mom would drop me off on Saturday morning. I had money for a few hours' ride on a rental horse. The people running the stable would take pity on me and let me take out Prince, a piebald pinto gelding who scared most people. He had learned to rear up and paw the air until the person would jump off and give up. I just stayed on until he got tired of that, and then ask him to go forward. He would eventually. We would ride around the flight line for hours. Just him and me. I had lots of time to dream and think of many things. I was lonely though.

That close bond with the equine family had started when Dad had taught me to read. Dogs have always been an important part of my life, and still are. Yet, horses are magic! They are a great love of mine. We have a great heart connection My parents let me start riding lessons at age five. Hmm, soon after The Closet. Was Mom making up for something? There had been a CBF riding stable on that base also. They had lessons for little kids. My memory has me on a beautiful steed, running like the wind up and down the hills! I found an old photo once. There I was, a smiling little curly-headed girl, on a horse with its head practically on the ground! The horse was ancient, and so tired. But to me, she was fabulous! Wherever we moved, they let me take riding lessons. Finally, in Puerto Rico, the cost was low enough for me to have my own horse. I filled the hole in my heart with horses. By high school there were eight horses under my care. They were my best buddies! I was at the stable all day in the summer, and after school during the academic year.

I was always aloof with friends. I had few friends and never liked being part of a larger group. The moving every two years with my Dad's work reinforced this. The first thing a kid whose parent is in the service does when going to a new school is to verify the "rotation date" of prospective friends. This lets you know who will be around for a while. The "rotation date" is when their family is going to move. Every military kid is well aware of that date!

When I was younger, I used to lament that I was from nowhere. Then, once my spiritual life began, I realized that I was from everywhere! Just give me a map, and anyplace could be home and comfortable. I could find my way around, anywhere in the world.

My first real long-lasting relationships came after Dad retired in Puerto Rico. I attended school from seventh to twelfth grade at Ramey High School on Ramey Air Force Base. Nixon closed the base in 1972, and the Coast Guard took over part of the base and kept the school open. Some of my best friends today are from that time. I do still have the attitude of "see you later" that I established with the relocations, and I'm not too good about staying in touch. Isn't that more the way of the world now? We do have to try to keep in touch, and make time for our friends.

One of my deepest connections in life is to Puerto Rico itself. After all the moving (we had lived in five different states and Okinawa), and never even seeing where I was born (we moved when I was six months old), Puerto Rico became a great love of my life. We moved to the island, the last of the Greater Antilles in the Caribbean, the Island of Enchantment, when I was eleven years old. It was the first place we had ever lived off base. The first time not living in military housing. It was cool to have a unique house. A real home!

My paternal grandparents were from Puerto Rico, and there has always been a deep connection to the island. Especially to certain beaches, and to the mountains. The mountains in Puerto Rico are magic, especially those where my paternal grandfather had been born and raised. When I am there my heart sings! I am jovial, and I can't help the giggles and laughter that emerge spontaneously from my heart.

On one of my last visits, some friends who own an organic coffee plantation invited me to stay. They introduced me to a mountain man in his late 70s who still cut racimos (the entire branch of a banana or plantain tree, with all the bunches of fruit from that one tree) for a living. He was known for his ability to go through a plantation of banana or plantain trees, cut the racimo branches, and bring them up from the depths of the valley to the top of the ridges, where the trucks could pick them up. He was thin and short. Serious in demeanor, and very humble. He lived in a small wooden home, made of sheets of tongue-and-groove plywood, unpainted. The only things on his walls were a paper calendar, with a picture of Jesus in the clouds above a circle of the "fallen" people playing cards and drinking whiskey, and a picture of a niece and nephew.

We spoke of his work, and I suggested using a horse to carry the racimos up to the top of the ridges. He chuckled, and said they were too much trouble. The ridges were so steep, the horses often fell and he would have to go down and bring them up. "The horses are too much work! I'd rather carry the crop up the hills myself!" He has been doing this all his life. That is connection to the land!

When I am in the mountains of Puerto Rico, I always have profound spiritual experiences, and visitations from the spirits of my ancestors. The connection to that land is in my soul. Whenever I return to the island, tears well up in my eyes at my first sight of the green mountains of the interior. I didn't work to make the connection. It just is. The connection is in my soul.

CHAPTER 3

The Master of Abuse

"The greater the power,
the more dangerous the abuse."
— EDMUND BURKE

He knows, he knows. He senses it like the animal that he is. The animal wants to eat. He eats energy. He sucks the life out of unsuspecting little ones. He wants the innocence. He wants to gnaw on their bones as he pleasures himself. This is an insatiable appetite. He needs to pleasure himself. The best way is with little ones. He can feed on their fear and their soft, soft flesh and the innocence. They are not tainted with their own desires and wishes. They are ready to swallow whole, and melt-in-the-mouth savory! Yum! A tasty little one come to suck and be sucked. To eat and be eaten. The insatiable desire of consuming the life force of the young innocent is uncontrollable. He is the master. He sits on his throne and tells the others tales of intrigue and shows them how to do it. How to teach the little ones. How to draw them to him so he can use and abuse them. He gets great pleasure out of teaching his trade to the new apprentice abusers.

They are young and vulnerable, too. The only requisite is that they have the same animal desire to consume the young. He used to go out and find them, the little ones. He used to be free to go out and seek them from family and friends. Then he got found out. He hurt the wrong one and he got found out. Now he can't go out and get the little ones himself. He needs his minions to do that for him. He now finds minions that are older than the little ones, but still naive about the ways of the world. They are incentivized to seek the master's help for the things they want. He starts with getting them alcohol, and befriends them. He lets them come to drink at his place. He makes his place their safe place. Then he teaches them how to smoke pot. Once he has them under the influence and comfortable he starts with the sex stuff. He lets them use his place for sex, and entices them to let him watch and touch. Then he shows them the pictures of him with the little ones. Little by little, he shows them the way to teach a little one to feel safe. How to make the secret play easy and fun. He shows how to gain the trust and confidence of the little ones. He gets them excited about the little ones, and their innocence, and their energy. Their life force that is raw and full. How the little ones will do what one wants when trust is gained. Then he begins to have his minions bring the little ones to him. They have been trained to listen. Both the minions and the little ones. The little ones trust the minions. They are family or trusted people of the family. The child has been trained to obey, and so cannot resist. Then, when the minions finally bring the little child to the master, they are unable to resist. They are afraid of the master, but they cannot resist. They are afraid, and the minions change into threatening scary strangers who want to watch the master use and abuse the little ones. The master feeds on the flesh and Soul of the little ones and the minions learn to do the same. It is terror for the little ones. Terror to be there and terror that they will be left there. Never to return to the loving home where they feel safe and cared for by their loving parents. The greatest fear is that if they do not do what the master wants, if they do not submit and allow whatever violation he performs on them, they will never go home again. It might never end! The little ones learn to submit and to allow. Their little souls hover above their bodies, waiting for it to be over. Waiting for the chance to return home. They learn to leave the body when touch is applied to their little bodies. They leave the shell of a body and wait to return when it is safe. When the master and his minions have had their fill for today. Then the little one's soul can return to the body, broken and weak. "I won't tell anyone! Please take me home! I want to go home!"

CHAPTER 4

Loved or Unlovable

"If you want to be loved,
be lovable"
— Ovid

The little girl felt she was unloved and unlovable. I thought my mom didn't like me much. She always sent me away. Away from the kitchen. Away from helping her. "You can't do this!" she would say. "You're too little and you don't know how. Besides, I'd have to do it over again!" Always she sent me away from her. Was it because I was bad? Was I just no good? Was that why she didn't want me around?

I feel the hurt and and loneliness in my chest right now as I remember the way I felt.

Was little Toni afraid to feel because of the abuse? Was she unloved and unlovable because of the abuse or because of the response to the abuse when she finally told the secret? Both to be sure! The multitude of feelings were overwhelming! So much to be suppressed. So much feeling about both the abuse and the confusion about what little Toni had done wrong. "Why did Mom get so upset with me? What is wrong with me?"

Most of my life was spent in avoiding the feelings. Avoiding not feeling loved. The maternal family history of alcohol addiction paved the way for addictions of my own. Food – and sugar especially. Mom always had those great desserts! And always ready with them when she saw any kind of feelings were overwhelming me. Alcohol was next, from a very young age. I started drinking alcohol at thirteen. Rum was easily available to kids in Puerto Rico. If you were brave enough to go into the "Rum Shack" (small local bars) and had the $1.25 for the "caneca" (half pint) they would sell it to you. We would ride our horses to the Rum Shack and buy the "caneca" and some Cokes. We'd pour out half the Coke and fill it with rum. Thank goodness the horses knew the way back to the stable! Next was "pot" by fifteen. Couldn't get enough of that! My favorite high was rum and pot. That really did the trick! Couldn't feel anything at all! My favorite was the spinning feeling of both. Totally off my rocker. Little did I know that this behavior was an act of burying the pain. A pain that I did not consciously remember at all.

Being involved with using these substances never got in the way of my being on the Honor Roll, in the Honor Society and graduating high school in three years. Ninth and tenth grades at the same time, replacing study hall, art and music with more math, English and science. Talk about an overachiever! My senior thesis was on the medical benefits of meditation, Transcendental Meditation specifically. I had quit drinking alcohol and smoking pot by this time. I was determined to eliminate it from my life, but destined to return to it several times during life, always after emotional upsets, always involving love relationships.

This feeling of not feeling loved, of not even being lovable, haunts me to this day. Yet, occasionally, love does sneak into my heart. I have glimpses from family, friends and clients. Could it be that those promises the little girl made in The Closet have made such a lasting impression? Could the vow to never let anyone in, to never need anyone, be spilling over into my life now and preventing love and nourishment from getting in? Unfortunately, those promises made in a state of excitation get anchored in the nervous system. You can learn to make different choices, but these habitual responses have to be recognized and countered again and again. Countered with choices made from the place of what you want now. Of how I want to live my life now!

The strange thing is, I had a dream about the abuser. The one who had taken me to the master and the others. A dream where I loved him, and my having told the secret led to his banishment from my life. I missed him. I missed the attention he gave me. Did he miss me? He had only hurt me sometimes. Other times we had fun. Did he have to go? No one ever gave me attention like that again. I was never special to anyone like that again. I missed that energy he had for me, though it could be scary. How strange these memories! How did they fit into the misshapen container of my heart?

CHAPTER 5

Finding Purpose

*"Our prime purpose in this life
is to help others.
And if you can't help them,
at least don't hurt them."*

— DALAI LAMA

O n being asked the rather serious question in my junior year of high school, "What do you want to major in when you go to college?" held the ridiculous undertones of "What do you want to do for the rest of your life?" "Ride horses and go to the beach!" was my serious reply. We compromised on a two-year community college that offered both a Horse Management program (where I could learn all about training, feeding, breeding, riding and showing horses) and all the usual requisites for a freshman and then sophomore college student. I left my warm, tropical island home and headed out for Northwest Community College in Powell, Wyoming. This small Mormon town is situated twenty miles from Cody, the gateway to Yellowstone National Park. "The surfer girl heads to the mountains" is the name of this tale. The first fall, walking on campus across the beautiful green lawns, we had to walk around a new fence that workers were putting up. "Why on earth would they be putting fences across the fields?" I exclaimed. "They are for the drifts," a friend from Wyoming explained. "Drifts? What are drifts?" was my naive reply. "Snow drifts, silly!" she explained. I had no idea! I even believed in jackalopes for my first six months in Wyoming! These are the fabled cross between jackrabbits and antelopes. They can be seen stuffed in local curio shops, hence my belief in them. However, for all you out there who are believers, they are not real. Who knew?

It was a long first year away from home, with snow and wind that left me in tears. "No one has to live like this!" I would cry. "There are much nicer places to live and ride horses!" I survived the winter. Walking the mile and a half to the stable by 6 AM, blizzard or not. The feed barn was only open for fifteen minutes, and if you weren't there, your horse did not eat. We had been assigned horses that needed to be retrained for the first semester. They had been donated by the local ranchers. This was a win/win situation, for both the ranchers and the school. My mare was so difficult that once the riding instructor told me to get off and let her show me how "to make that mare work!" She gave the horse back to me after a fifteen-minute struggle, with a "Good luck!" The instructor had thought that I was not able to handle her sufficiently. Well, the horse was just an overworked, ruined mare.

We were well disciplined. Cleaning the stalls (poop and wet sawdust) by hand with gloves and a five-gallon paint bucket. Only allowed to use a wheelbarrow and shovel on the weekends so as not to waste sawdust. We had to ride daily, and could not wear gloves no matter how cold it was! Coming from Puerto

Rico, this was unbearable. "No gloves: you can't feel the horse's mouth. And no trail riding! You kids are just goofing off!" These people took my love of horses and turned it inside out! I had some of the first headaches of my life trying my best to ride well for them.

The second semester, we got a three-to-five-year-old horse straight off the high range that had never been touched by human hands. They had rounded them up and herded them into a truck with a chute, and then put them in a stall at the stable with a chute. It took me over an hour to catch my three-year-old quarter horse mare in the stall! We were responsible for teaching them everything from first touch to wearing a saddle, and give them their first experiences being ridden. We even cold-shoed our own horses under the tutelage of the local farrier. We used a round pen with a deep, soft dirt base. This way the young wild horses tired quickly, and it was a softer landing when we were bucked off. We actually rode the horses in a horse show at the end of the semester. Victory was sweet!

That first year in Wyoming was hard. I was an outsider with my surfer girl looks, and a knowledge of life that the ranch and farm girls in the program could never imagine. That school broke my resolve, and I decided to transfer to the University of Wyoming at Laramie to take up geological engineering. I figured that it was much better to have a good job and leave horses as a hobby. Besides, math and science were a breeze.

I spent the following year at U. of W. and then transferred to University of Arizona. Enough of those cold, windy winters already! I kept up with the twenty-four-credit schedule, and experienced first hand how stress caused serious physical illness. My heart palpitations were such a problem that a visit to the university hospital was in order. My EKG and physical exam were normal. The doctor set me down and asked, "What classes are you taking this semester?" "Calculus 3, Physics, Thermodynamics, Mineralogy, Cartography (my personal favorite!), Organic Chemistry, among others," was my matter-of-fact reply. "Well! I think you need to drop at least three of those!" he exclaimed. "You are driving yourself to an early grave at age nineteen!" It was then that I realized that the palpitations coincided with the Wednesday Calculus quiz and the Friday Physics quiz. No wonder! I dropped both of those. It was then that I realized, after three years in the geological engineering field, that I hated the topic. I wanted to help people – not look for oil! There was no way I could stay on in this field. Besides, marrying my boyfriend looked like a better option. My parents cried when I called to tell them. I quit school, married and tried to settle down. It was agony! A little over a year later we divorced.

Returning to my beloved Puerto Rico and a life of leisure, there were easy jobs, lots of beach time and horses. Barb (my high school sailing friend) and I started a food-buying coop, Survival Foods. We had both become vegetarians, and there weren't many options for organic food on the island. We bought our food from Magnolia Warehouse in Atlanta, Georgia. They invited me up to observe their cooperative operation, and to check out Sevananda Coop in Little Five Points of Atlanta. We went to a cooperative conference for a weekend, and my eyes were opened to a whole new world. Consensus was their means of making decisions, and these people lived their beliefs.

"If you think this was fun, you should come with us to the Rainbow Gathering!" one of the Magnolia Warehouse people invited after the conference. I had never heard of these famous gatherings that take place in National Forests, usually in the West, every summer. This was the only event held in the East. It was in West Virginia, and we could drive. I went with the Atlanta contingency. Barb went from Ohio State University, where she was attending college.

This is an amazing happening. People come from all over the country. The core group of the Rainbow Family arrives several months early, so as to prepare the forest for tens of thousands of people over the Fourth of July weekend. They build outhouses and start growing seedling trees to replant after all the campers leave. The Family stays after everyone else goes home to return the forest to its natural, pre-Gathering state. Each group of people makes a small camp for themselves and offers some service to the whole community for free. My dreams of utopia from high school were being fed! There were three meals a day served at the main central camp, and other camps supplied tea, or popcorn, or music, or volleyball, or storytelling. It was amazing!

One day, after hearing a grandson of Black Elk speak the history of his people, I was wandering through the meadow. There was a huge line of people, so I strolled over and asked someone what they were in line for. "There are chiropractors giving free adjustments!" a woman excitedly told me. "What is a chiropractor?" was my innocent reply. "Just get in line, it is wonderful! You'll love it!" So, I joined the line and met new friends. As we approached the awnings under which the chiropractors were working, I saw brochures from Life Chiropractic College. "The body heals itself with the Life Force that flows within it," the brochure stated. "Wow! I believe this also," I thought to myself. I still remembered how I used to make up stories when I was eight years old to explain for myself how the body worked.

One story I found written in a journal spoke of little people who lived in each part of the body. They communicated by calling out to each other. "Here comes the food!" the mouth people would call to the stomach people. They did the work that kept the body functioning. I learned later in chiropractic college that those "little people" were the nerves and other organizing systems of the body.

Finally, I reached the front of the line and I was next. All at once, a great wind began to blow and everyone's tents started blowing away, including mine! I ran to get my tent and reinforce its tiedowns, then went inside for the duration of the rainstorm that followed the great wind. I never went back to get my treatment that day, or the rest of the weekend. But I had that brochure!

I wore the brochure thin, reading and re-reading the words. I looked up chiropractic in the dictionary and in the encyclopedia. (There was no Internet in those days.) There were no chiropractors Puerto Rico. There was one on St. Thomas, but when I called, his answering machine said, "Hello! The office is closed until November. Please call back at that time." The invitation to come study at Life Chiropractic College near Atlanta was irresistible. I decided to apply. I had received the brochure in July and sent my application in August. The acceptance letter arrived in November. All the requirements necessary (the equivalent of a bachelor's degree in science) were fulfilled by my three years in engineering school. The only thing lacking was a human biology class with a lab: three hours. Though I had never heard the word Chiropractic, somehow I had satisfied almost all the prerequisites. Leaving home in January, I made the move to Marietta, Georgia. First task: human biology with a lab, and then chiropractic college would begin in April. The first class that spring was philosophy with Dr. Rabin. Sitting there that first day, listening with great enthusiasm, the thought came to me: "I was born for this!" And never have I looked back.

In the first quarter, a classmate tapped my shoulder one day. "See that guy up there in front? He has never even been adjusted! Can you imagine, coming to school here and never having been to a chiropractor!" "No, I can't imagine it." I replied quietly. Being in the same situation myself, I realized it was time to remedy that. Each student needs to first find themselves a student doctor, and then start receiving care in the clinic on campus. I decided on a studious, serious upperclassman.

On my first visit to the clinic, after he had examined me and determined what he would do, it was time for the adjustment. The student doctor then stands in the hallway and waits for one of the clinic doctors to come and review the plan and observe the adjustment. My student doctor, David, stood waiting a little impatiently. "Oh, darn it!" he exclaimed under his breath. "The clinic doctor who is coming is such a jerk! I'll be sure to do my best so he doesn't take over and adjust you. He is very rough, and he has hurt some other clients of mine!" I started getting nervous as my clinician, David, started to sweat, with wet spots forming under his armpits, turning the light blue jacket required by the clinic to a darker shade. The clinic doctor approached and took my file to examine it. He looked at me – and my jaw dropped! There stood the man who was going to adjust me at the Rainbow Gathering! He did have clothes on now, but I had gotten a good look at his face that day before the wind had started blowing. If he had adjusted me that day, and if he had been rough with me, as David had just warned, I would never have started this journey! I would never have been inclined to study chiropractic. Spirit certainly was looking out for me that day – and many times before and after! Verification came after the visit, when David, after we left the clinic, reported, "Can you believe that guy! He actually went with a group of people to the Rainbow Gathering last year and was giving adjustments in the nude! Now he has revealed his true self, and he is so cruel with all the students!"

The motto of Life Chiropractic College is: "To Give, To Love and To Serve". This motto is called The Lasting Purpose. This became my motto too, and the quest on which I embarked through school, my internship and my first practice in Puerto Rico. I am still fulfilling my Lasting Purpose. Thank you Sid Williams, D.C., founder of Life Chiropractic College, now know as Life University.

CHAPTER 6

The Quest

*"The eternal quest of the individual human
being is to shatter his loneliness."*
— Norman Cousins

The quest that began at birth found its full expression in Chiropractic. Here was a way I could help others and receive from them gratitude and respect. Here was a way to create the interaction that I craved so deeply – that I needed to feed my soul.

The outpatient clinic at Life Chiropractic College opened at 7 AM, and I was there every day. The reception desk had a sign-up sheet for those students, like myself, who wanted to serve the "walk-in's," those who didn't have a student doctor yet. This was the way to learn how to build rapport with new people and see all kinds of cases. The learning curve was steep – and priceless! There was also an x-ray department where students could volunteer to take the x-rays and read them with the radiologist. This served me very well. My office in Puerto Rico would have its own x-ray machine, and this was the place to learn about taking the films, developing them and then reading them. Excelling in these two clinics proved invaluable.

I spent all the breaks between quarters in the last two years of school in Davenport, Iowa at the clinic of Dr. Larry J. Troxell. He was one of twelve doctors taught by Dr. Clarence Gonstead, founder of the Gonstead Technique, one of the foundational chiropractic techniques taught at all chiropractic colleges worldwide. This structural technique addresses not only the misalignment of every joint in the body, but the relationship of the autonomic nervous system to the patient's symptoms.

Upon graduation, I returned to Puerto Rico to open my own office in Aguadilla, on the northwestern corner of the island. There were no other chiropractors on that end of the island, as most of the others were in the San Juan area. In fact, I was the third woman to receive a chiropractic license in Puerto Rico. Working with Dr. Troxell had prepared me to open my own practice at age twenty-six. I modeled my office after his, and I combined the Lasting Purpose motto of Life Chiropractic College and that of Dr. T, "It is your duty to see as many people as you can, in the most effective way possible."

This determined woman was off and running! Just putting the sign up on the main road, two blocks from the regional hospital, attracted clients immediately. No advertising necessary! By the end of the first year I had three full-time secretaries, with 350 patient visits a week. Working long hours allowed me to treat seventy people a day! I did all the exams, and the x-rays (taking, developing and reading them) by myself. All the spinal adjusting was done by hand. No physical therapy machines or other modalities. Within a few years, massage therapy offered by a certified massage therapist was added to the services. Massage always came after the adjustment, so the patients knew that my work was the primary treatment.

There were struggles to get the office open. First, getting the license to practice Chiropractic. Then, facing the many obstacles to a young, single woman getting the necessary permits. "The doctor has to be here," many a secretary told me. "I *am* the doctor!" I repeated, many times, to get access to supervisory offices for permits to have the x-ray machine and to operate a medical office.

Finally the office was open, the sign out front – and the people started coming in. One of the initial problems was that the high school Spanish class had not really taught me how to form proper sentences on my own. Those first intake examinations began with, *"Dolor? Donde?"* which means, "Pain? Where?" In the cases of disc injury, I would follow up that initial question by asking, *"Dolor cuando...* (sneeze and cough) which is "Pain when..." and I would then sneeze and then cough. Disc injury causes pain on coughing and sneezing, and also straining in an effort to evacuate. I dared only act out the first two. People would look at me quizzically and then either nod or shake their heads in response to this strange inquiry by the young doctor. Those with the pain knew exactly what the question was about. Those unfortunate initial clients had to sit through the history taking, examination, and x-rays. Then, a thirty-minute explanation of the x-rays and the proposed treatment plan in my broken Spanish. When they agreed to treatment we struck a deal, "I'll fix your back, and you'll teach me to speak properly, okay?" *"Si, si!"* was the usual reply. People are so willing to help when you ask them! During the long days, there would be focus on a few words. I'd keep asking those same words until I remembered, and tried to use them often until they stuck in my mind. When the office first opened, it was *"Americana, eh?"* and after three years, people would ask what country in South America I was from. The Puerto Rican accent was incorrect, but the pronunciation allowed me to slip by under the guise of some foreign accent.

Quite a few cases that presented in my office in Puerto Rico were problems that many chiropractors do not see in their entire career. In the U.S., patients with spina bifida, or those with neurologic disease or paralysis, would never go to a chiropractor. In Puerto Rico however, my reputation of having heart and a wish to help all people, along with a good success rate in difficult cases, led people to come to my office with a wide range of ailments. Ambulance attendants carried in people with disc ailments weekly. In Puerto Rico, the ambulances are private companies, so people having extreme pain will call to be taken to the doctor. "People get carried in – and they walk out!" was the report from patients and their family members. The word spread and my practice grew.

Knowing that the people needed to learn alternative choices, we started offering classes through the office, which I taught for the most part. "Learn to cook brown rice and use natural sweeteners," and "How to grow sprouts for nutrition" were several of these classes. They always led to comical situations, due to my lack of vocabulary in Spanish to discuss and teach the topics. One memorable occasion was my sending a letter to over 500 people for the cooking class. The high school on the nearby military base had agreed to let me use their high-tech kitchen. The cooking classroom had a mirror, allowing the participants to see the counter and stove from the classroom. This is standard now, but then it was one of the only two on the island. Unfortunately, I neglected to have one of the Spanish-speaking secretaries proofread the letter. On asking people if they had received the invitation letter for the class, they would smile, or snicker, "Oh yes!" Finally, on asking one of the staff, she reluctantly told me that the letter said, "Come join me to eat me with brown rice." I was mortified, and the joke was good for years. And it still is! When the fifty-plus people arrived for the class and got settled, everyone was anxious to learn about brown rice and how to cook it. Some had tried, and it just hadn't come out well like the white rice they were used to cooking. Well, the fact that my vocabulary on cooking was completely lacking hadn't become apparent to me, even after the letter fiasco! As the cooking lesson began, I reached for the pot to place it on the stove to boil the water and... didn't have the words for a lot of those things! I lifted the pot in the air and said "First you put the water in the..." "*Olla!*" yelled the group of students, teaching me the word for "pot." "Then you place it on the stove with twice the amount of water as rice. Then you heat the water to..." "*Hervir!*" they cried out, teaching me the word for "boil." It was quite the evening class! A new phrase needed to be added for classes and lectures, "I'm going to teach you about health and you can help me learn Spanish!" This always led to laughter and instant rapport with the audience.

My first years in practice revealed that there was a huge emotional component to symptoms, especially pain. This led to my search for further education. Neurolinguistic Programming (NLP) was one of my first fields of additional study. It was during this year-long course that the destructive and malicious nature of my own self-talk first revealed itself. As part of the NLP training, we would practice on each other. Discovering the litany of constant abuse in my head led me to wonder how I had ever been able to graduate from chiropractic college. How any success in life had been possible. I drove myself constantly with harsh words, and I held any sense of accomplishment far at bay. This led me to begin developing an encouraging pleasant voice in my head to counter the mean one. While I was saying something mean to myself, the other voice would chime in, "That wasn't very nice!" Eventually, when I did something that would have led to retribution from the mean, judging voice, the nice voice would just automatically say, "I love you, Toni!" even without coaxing. This was a great evolutionary step for me. NLP did not gel well with my practice, but this transformation of my self-talk, and some other changes in communication skills with others, were well worth the training.

A skill that began to emerge naturally was intuition. The pace of the practice led something within me to seek assistance from other sources. The Source within started to speak to me in the form of knowing which area of the spine to work with, or what to say when and to whom. I always double checked with the science and chiropractic tools, but that inner voice was always right. Then, a regular patient came in, begging me to see his brother: "You've helped so many in our family. Please see him, he is in extreme pain! We know you can help him!" Right away, my gut said "Don't do it!" I had no idea why. Thinking it was just because I was so busy, I said, "I couldn't possibly see him until late Thursday night." "Wonderful! We will bring him then." My gut started to do flips. "Be sure to bring all the x-rays and reports from the other doctors he has seen." "Of course!" he stated.

When the day came for the examination my stomach continued with the dance. "What is going on!" I thought. I asked all the appropriate questions in the man's history to rule out any reason to refer. I carefully reviewed all x-rays and other testing; examining the prior films and taking new ones of my own. There was nothing that showed he should not be accepted as a patient. When I administered the structural adjustment to his spine, he would cry out in pain. Now, often the structural adjustment (when the chiropractor moves the bone with force) can be uncomfortable, but this was extreme. After three treatments, I decided to tell him I could not continue to see him. He didn't come to his next appointment. When my secretary called to check on him, she was told that he was in the hospital with lung cancer, which had metastasized to the spine – right in the area where I had been adjusting him! I went to the hospital to visit. He was pale and had an oxygen mask. He moved it aside and said, "Thank you for trying to help me!" My heart broke. "You're welcome!" He died a few days later. I vowed to not only always listen to my intuition when it spoke to me, but to develop it to be a reliable tool in all cases. This seed has grown into a great asset, which I now share with all my clients and teach to others.

Other evolutionary changes occurred, as I read thought-provoking books by Deepak Chopra, Larry Dossey, Norman Cousins, Wayne Dyer and many others. Trainings in basic shamanism and heart-centered living broadened my scope of thinking and feeling. Rubenfeld Synergy Method training, and the journey that began there, will follow in other chapters.

The wounds of my youth; the need to constantly prove myself. The need for approval, and to be of service to others, allowed me to excel – and to assist thousands of people over the nine years my chiropractic office operated in Aguadilla, Puerto Rico. The wound had turned into a gift – and it had blossomed.

There were many rewards, the trust of the people being the most valuable. The precious accomplishment of all the experience gained by seeing so many people in such a short amount of time. There were months that seemed to bring all types of specific problems of a certain area of the body. One month it was knees: golfer knees, surfer knees, old lady knees, childhood baseball knees, runner's knees, etc. etc. Then would come discs and then shoulders and then ankles. There was no end to the learning afforded me in this practice. Another reward was the recognition by other experts and colleagues. I was even appointed by the Governor to the Puerto Rico Board of Chiropractic Examiners: the first woman to hold this position.

CHAPTER 7

From a Rut to Rubenfeld

*"The only difference between a rut and
a grave are the dimensions."*
— ELLEN GLASGOW

M y interest in learning more about the mental/emotional component of healing led me to attend the IONS conference in Washington, D.C. in 1993. Three full days of workshops with some of the most famous healers and teachers of the time. There were so many wonderful choices. It was amazing to experience! I chose to attend presentations by Caroline Myss and Ilana Rubenfeld. There were others, but these two were the most interesting to me. My main memory of the entire weekend were those two sessions – and Deepak Chopra spoke as the opening speaker.

Deepak Chopra's first books on health and healing were a catalyst for my journey towards integrating different modalities. The ideas he and Bernie Siegel presented were a window into a new world for me: how thought and emotion could affect health. When Deepak spoke that first day, he impressed me. He began speaking and without notes, he outlined his topic, spoke of all its aspects, and circled around back to the start. A complete package of ideas presented in a concise and succinct way, and exactly on time. An example for me to aspire to as a speaker and teacher, still to this day!

Another famous teacher seemed tough, cynical and cold. She asked for a volunteer from the audience. She began to give him a reading of his energy field, and the volunteer was quickly wishing he hadn't. She read his chakras and told him that others were using him, and that he needed to stop the drain from his third chakra before he got ill. That when he did change and began to speak up for himself, all those around him would soon leave him. His girlfriend was sitting beside him. The teacher asked if she was with him, and then said, "Well, she'll be leaving you soon enough!" Everyone in the audience laughed, but he was mortified. I felt so sorry for him!

Ilana Rubenfeld, on the other hand, had humor and grace. She was speaking about the limbic system, and the practitioner's need for self care. The office in Puerto Rico was eating me alive, and she was speaking of something I desperately needed in my life. She had my complete attention and interest. The emotional content, and how it affected our body/mind, was part of my quest. I was intensely interested in how to meld these new ideas into my practice. In one exercise, participants were partnered up, and we talked and introduced ourselves. Then we closed our eyes, rubbed our hands together, and slowly touched hands. It was amazing to feel the field of the other as his hands approached mine. I didn't know my partner before this exercise. Then Ilana led us through feeling certain emotions, and using movement and touch to express these emotions to each other without words. One at a time. It was amazing to actually get to know this person through touch, not words. He became alive to me, and I felt we were sharing in a most personal way. It was almost embarrassing at times, because through the touch and movement, I knew I could not hide who I really was. The choices I made and the way I touched would reveal me to him. No blinders. No barriers. How could I hide now?

It was amazing. Then Ilana asked us to realize what we now knew about this person. What had not been realized from our five-minute speaking conversation. Using our touch, and not using our eyes, was revealing him to me, and me to him, on a totally new horizon. This was fascinating! She led us through other exercises that were equally exciting, but that one stands out. Another amazing point was that she was leading us, through experience, toward what she wanted us to know, instead of telling us through lecture and Power Point. We were actually experiencing in our bodies what it was that she wanted to teach. Fascinating! This is how I teach now: through experience first, then with discussion to draw out the lessons.

At this point, she asked for a massage table to be brought out, and for a volunteer. She asked people to arrange their chairs in a circle. As we did so, my former partner looked at me and said, "She is going to choose you." "No, not me! There are so many others who want the chance to be on the table now." "Yes, you!" he exclaimed.

They brought the table out and set it right in front of us. We were in the center of the audience, with more than 200 people watching. She asked for a volunteer and about thirty of us raised our hands. She looked to me and said, "You can come up, my dear." I was so surprised. I went up to the table and sat on it as she indicated. Little did I know that she was going to change my life forever!

"What is motivating you to come up to the table today?" Ilana said. "I am a chiropractor and I've been in practice for eight years in Puerto Rico," I began to explain. "I've been working twelve-hour days, seeing 350 clients a week, and I am so burned out. I have to make a change, and I can't seem to do it. I need help." Before coming to the IONS Conference, I had started having dreams of a horned monster chasing me – and I had come to realize that the monster was of my own creation, and that it was my office! I knew I had to change. To leave the office. I had tried to make changes several times, to no avail.

"Oh my! You certainly are busy!" Ilana explained. Then she asked me to lie down on the table, face up. I did. She gently touched my head. Her hands were so soft! "You are very fragile at this point in your life." It wasn't a question. How did she know that? Tears welled up in my eyes as I nodded my head in agreement. My throat constricted with surprising ferocity. What was wrong with me? She walked quietly to my feet and touched me there. She rocked my feet from side to side. "You like to walk, don't you?" she asked with a confident tone, knowing the answer already. "I do!" was my reply. She gently and quietly slid one hand under a hip, and she placed her other hand gently on the top of my hip. "Tell me about your office," she directed.

"I love to help people," and I went into describing my mission.

As I spoke, she gently asked questions or made comments, and moved around the table, touching or holding various places on my body. The 200 people in the room disappeared for me. They might reappear occasionally when someone coughed or laughed at some comment we made in our dialogue. Then they would all disappear again as if we were in our own bubble. I was deep in another state of consciousness. Somewhere else. She was with me, but unobtrusive, and unconditionally accepting of whatever I said. She led me through some visualizations. She ended up having me make choices, like from a Chinese restaurant menu, in my mind. One thing from column A, one from column B, and one from column C. What did I want on my plate? This was so creative and unexpected, it allowed me space to choose how I wanted my life to be. Not what I wanted for others, but what I wanted for me. I had never considered that!

By the end of the session I knew I could leave the office and Puerto Rico, to start a new way of being with people that did not require me to take total responsibility for the outcome of their lives.

I did sell my practice. That was another miracle in and of itself. I went from not knowing how I would ever be able to leave it, to knowing what to do and doing it. I went home to Puerto Rico, and within a few weeks wrote a letter saying that my practice was for sale. The letter was sent to all the chiropractic colleges in the U.S., and the day they were sent, I received a phone call. It was from a chiropractor in Canada. Of course there was no way the letters had even left the island yet! God was in charge, and because I showed that I was finally ready to leave the office by taking the action step with the letters, God guided this chiropractor to call me. He was calling me to ask if I knew of anyone who might have a practice for sale! He was married to a Puerto Rican woman whose parents lived close to my office, and they wanted to move to Puerto Rico to be close to them. "Yes!", I almost shouted. Inwardly I thought, "Is this a joke!"

He ended up coming to Puerto Rico, following me around the office for several months, and buying the entire office from me.

All the case files, furniture and equipment. Even the secretaries stayed to continue being a part of the team. He was blessed by the opportunity, and I was so relieved! After my last day at the office, I took the office copies of all the receipts from the nine years home with me – and burned them. What an identity crisis! Who am I if I am not Dr. Rivera? A whole new chapter of my life began! One of my first steps was to take the Rubenfeld Synergy Method training with Ilana Rubenfeld.

The Rubenfeld training was amazing. From the first night, entering into the brownstone in Greenwich Village, New York, I knew life would never be the same. Here was a group of curious seekers, of whom I was one. Excitement, joy, humor and aliveness! A young man greeted me entering the building and said: "Leave your shoes here, and this is where you will leave them for the entire week." He was obviously as nervous and excited as I was. "Can't I wear them home tonight!?" was my jovial reply. He was embarrassed in that moment, but would soon give me some powerful teachings. He was one of the teaching assistants, and actually my small-group leader. I hadn't meant to embarrass him, but I couldn't resist!

We all traipsed down the staircase to what was the living room, dining room and kitchen of this New York brownstone. There was lovely art on the walls and a large decorative door, two sided, hand carved in India. The fireplace had a large painting of a wise old Chinese man in a blue and white robe. How many times I would gaze at him in wonder, and reflect on the magic that was occurring before his eyes in this room. The Persian rug was a garden of flowers. This was a home and a wonderful temple for the learning of body/mind/emotions/spirit magic. Ilana had created a wondrous place for people to come for growth and learning. To heal and be healed in this brownstone that had once been called "The House of Love" in the '60s. This was the beginning of an era of change and growth for me that has lasted to this day! I spent the first four years of that journey in that brownstone, with Ilana and her team.

That first week was a shock. We would sit in a group and have discussions, which to me seemed pointless. Who cares what these people think? I want to learn from Ilana. I don't care what these imbeciles think! Who cares, really, how these people feel. How they are affected by what they have seen or learned. There was one woman who always talked and talked, on and on. I wished she would shut up! When I shared anything, reluctantly, I always made sure to know exactly what I was going to say before I spoke. Concise and to the point! No rambling into the feelings I was having! What feelings? I had a lot to learn about sharing, and how those sharing sessions led to people's deepest realizations about themselves and the world.

When we met in small groups, in the upper rooms that had once been bedrooms, we began to practice contact. Real contact. Something I had never truly experienced, though I had been touching thousands of people for years. In one of the exercises, we were in pairs, with one person lying on the table as client, and the other standing as the synergist. The synergist would approach the table, pause, and then move back. We did this again and again. Then the teacher, the young man who had told me to leave my shoes by the door all week, added touching the head with our fingertips once the synergist approached the table. It was tedious and boring. What was this supposed to do with how Ilana worked?

When it was time to share in the small group at the end of the two hours, I had to say it. "What are you supposed to do when someone comes into your office, dragging a leg and screaming in pain?" I was exasperated! There was no way that this could help the kind of cases I was seeing! What a waste of time! After a pause, "Send them to a chiropractor!" the teacher replied with a smile. He got me that time! Boy, did I have a lot to learn!

As the training continued, I had many internal struggles. "What was happening? What was I doing here? Didn't they want to relieve people's pain? Weren't we supposed to be learning how to take care of people's pain? What good was this, what was it for, if it was not to relieve someone's pain?"

I came to understand that the point was to explore the client's life. To explore what the body was saying. To explore the body's point of view of their lives. In this way, it was like teaching someone to fish instead of giving them fish. This was the point.

I remember being with Ilana at a five-day workshop in Boulder, Colorado, some years after the training. One of the young men who had volunteered to come up to the table said he'd volunteered because he had low-back pain. He wanted relief! What would she say now? "Well, lets make an agreement. If your low back feels better after, great! If it doesn't, that is not what we are doing here anyway!" She smiled.

I could absolutely not believe she had told him that. How could she tell him she wasn't interested in, or even going to try to reduce his pain? This was amazing! She started as she always did, having him lie on his back, face up, on the table. She touched his head and then his feet. Meeting him where he was, and letting him know that she accepted him through her touch. This is of paramount importance. Acceptance, without judgment. The ultimate gift to any other person – and the ultimate goal when being with ourselves.

CHAPTER 8

Numb to Life

"A deep sense of love and belonging is
an irreducible need of all people."
— Brene Brown

I see now how I had become numb to life in many ways. Numb to my feelings. Numb to my body and its needs. I had become subservient to others whom I deemed necessary in my life. What did I need to do to have friends in elementary, middle and high school? Okay, that is what I did, all the while making it appear to myself and others as if it was my choosing. This created a weakness, over time, that manifested as indifference in my life. The weakness became manifested in my body as weakness in my right arm. This of course has a physical explanation: many accidents with horses where I landed on my head. Injury and permanent damage to my neck. But I know that it also had to do with the injury to my heart. Was that damage permanent? Was any of it permanent, or could both the physical and the emotional truly heal?

It interests me that rental horses have a type of numbness, a type of emotional defect in their heart. Their defect is that they don't feel loved or lovable. They don't have a person who is their own. They are being used for others' purposes. They are like abused children. I had never realized this, with all the rental horses I had ridden over the years. To me they were wonderful because they let me ride them. There was a relationship of sorts, and I definitely was a kind of abuser because I made them do my bidding. Just what had been done to me. Without realizing this, I had become like the abusers. Remember Prince, that piebald gelding at the CBF stable on the Air Force Base in South Carolina – my frequent mount when I was nine. He had the habit of rearing up on his hind legs so that people would be scared and jump off, leaving him alone. With me, he would rear up in the beginning of the ride. I would slap him on the neck and yell at him to cut it out. He would acquiesce, and we would go out and ride along the flight line for hours. I did love Prince, but I didn't really know him. His likes and dislikes. His needs. I loved him for serving my needs. Was that how the abuse was? They did use threats to make me stop resisting. Did the abuser care for me, and then use me to satisfy a need, just like I did with Prince?

These insights on horses came after buying a school horse from my dressage teacher. A school horse is more than a rental horse, because they are truly teachers, and they are treated with a lot more respect. My horse was named Willow. He was a Thoroughbred/ Quarter Horse cross, called an Appendix. He was twenty-two years old when I bought him, and he had quite a history. He had been a racehorse early on in his career. Nothing special, just one of those used on the track for warming up other horses. Probably to pace others who held more promise. He was bought from the track to be a hunter-jumper. He was then used for three-day eventing, the equestrian triathlon. The three days include dressage, arena jumping and cross-country jumping. Something had happened to him, and he had developed a large protrusion on his right shoulder. No one remembered what had happened to him. "Perhaps an accident where his trailer flipped," the vet had offered as a possibility. His owner ended up abandoning him at the stable. The owners of the stable put him out to pasture without any type of care. No vet, no farrier to clip his hooves, no grain. A dressage trainer found him and thought he was a good prospect for a school horse. She offered to take him off the barn owner's hands for the cost of what was due them. They agreed, and Willow found a home giving dressage lessons to little girls. Dressage is a very specific type of riding. You probably have seen people dressed in white jodhpurs and black top coats with tails, competing on television. That is dressage. The horses perform strict movements in very specific formats, and the riders don't seem to move at all. The directions are given by the rider with very slight movements of their various leg muscles and pelvis. Synchrony of horse and rider is the goal.

Willow was a very good teacher. If you gave the command correctly, he instantly responded. All of him: seventeen hands tall and at least a thousand pounds. If you did not give the command correctly, he completely ignored you. All of him. He was a big, beautiful boy with a heart of gold and the demeanor of a wise Buddhist master.

The woman trainer's clients had their own horses, for the most part, by the time I came on the scene. Usually I would have my lesson in the arena, maybe ride him out on the trail for a while, and then I would wash him off and brush him. Spoiling him a little. Then one day she said, "Leave Willow tied to the rail with his saddle on. Another woman is coming for a lesson after you." I was in shock. How could I leave him tied to the rail! He wouldn't get washed off and brushed. He wouldn't get his time being spoiled. The next day I asked her to buy him. She agreed and Willow became mine. Or, I should say, I became his! I was his little girl. He was my senior. The computation of horse years to people years is three of theirs to every one of ours. So he was twenty-two in people years, sixty-six in horse years. He had always shown affection to me, snuffling my pockets for the sugar cubes or carrots I had brought for him. But after I bought him, he knew we belonged to each other. I promised to care for him the rest of his life, and he gave me so much love. He nickered whenever he saw me. When I was sad or upset, he would put his muzzle next to my ear and blow gently, letting me know that he was there for me. He responded to my love, and taught me what love and respect for another being really was. The numbness in my heart started to melt. When it was raining, or windy and snowing, I would just sit in his stall with him. He would continue nickering for long periods. I would give him subtle body treatments (the same as I had developed for people) and he loved it. The first time his body began to respond to my touch, he swung his head around and looked at me in surprise, "What are you doing to me, girl!?" Then he melted. When I would work on his arthritic knees, he would lick my back. His spine became straight again, and his shoulder bulge disappeared. He looked like an eighteen-year-old horse. "I don't know what you are doing to that horse, but I sure hope someone takes care of me like you take care of him when I get to be his age!", the vet had remarked one day at Willow's routine check-up. I was able to ride him up to the end of his life. He would be so proud of us, perking himself up and moving with grace. He was almost thirty when he passed. That horse was one of the greatest loves of my life! He was instrumental in healing my numb and broken heart.

In writing this book now, in reflecting on the hurt done by the abuse – the injury to my love, to my heart – I realize that my mom's reaction to my telling her about the abuse was more harmful in the long term than the actual abuse itself. My brain somehow blocked memory of the abuse until I was an adult, and able to explore it. My response to her reaction, though, with her being unable to directly address my needs around the abuse, was the most formative occurrence in my life. Most importantly, she neglected to let me know that it was not my fault. That I had not done anything wrong. This was the most deeply harmful to me, because, at that young age, children believe that the world revolves around them. So, anything that happened – the abuse, her reaction to it, the energy of the response – was my fault. It changed my outlook on relationships, and how I fit in the world. She didn't realize it, but that interaction, and the abuse itself, had changed my ability to trust others in close relationships. This had left me alone in the world, even when I was with others.

CHAPTER 9

A Cyclic Pattern

*"Life is not so much about beginnings and
endings as it is about going on and on and on.
It is about muddling through the middle."*
— Anna Quindlen

There were ten years between my first marriage at age nineteen (divorced by twenty) and my second marriage at thirty. We were attracted to each other physically at first, and we married within six months of meeting. It lasted thirteen years. I had been determined to make it work, as he had at first. It was doomed to die from the beginning, though, as our marriage had no real ground to build on. We had a tumultuous relationship.

As I was already a chiropractor when we met, my addictions had been replaced by a new one. Workaholic syndrome. A meaning and purpose for life, Chiropractic! I didn't need the other ways of numbing out. I could now put all my energies and feelings into others. It was wonderful, being able to help so many people. Yet, I was lonely and felt alone. As I was looking for some connection, he seemed to be the one. He gave me the love and attention I needed, and we were good together in the beginning. With the office being so overwhelming, he helped on the home front and we started to make a home.

After three years, we moved to Santa Fe. There were many ups and downs. He helped me through my first memories of the abuse, and dealing with my overactive thyroid disease. He was understanding and supportive with regard to my going into the memories. Yet, he had his own problems. Struggles with his own inner demons. Perhaps the hurt in each of our hearts was part of what attracted us to each other in the first place! We hurt each other with our behaviors that arose from the inner turmoil. Finally, we gave up on the marriage. It had come down to my having to choose myself over him – the only choice possible really and not the first time I would face that choice. The theme of choosing my life and health was still hidden from my view at that point. Having to choose the divorce was one of the things that brought the theme to the surface.

After the divorce, I began to dedicate myself to me, and my health and well-being. A book about numerology spoke of my birth number being prone to moods (no joke!) and that I needed vigorous exercise. A light bulb went off. I had never tried that!

Starting with the treadmill, I worked up to five miles a day and felt great. Happy and enthusiastic, what I consider my true emotions! Becoming bored with the treadmill, I moved on to Bikram Yoga. What an amazing practice! Starting with a few times a week, I worked up to an almost daily practice. I was stronger than I had ever been in my life. Strong, flexible and fit! When I went to get a physical for life insurance, the nurse couldn't believe how fit I was for my age. I got the super-discounted price. Life was good. I was becoming the healthiest

I had ever been in my life. My meditation practice was going extremely well. My chiropractic practice had evolved to the body/mind/emotional/spiritual combination that fascinated me. My personal healing work with myself had progressed to the point where I was comfortable and accepting of myself in a way never possible in the past. New friend relationships were developing that were valuable to me. I had Willow, my horse love. The bliss of a balanced life was amazing. Unfortunately, it didn't last long.

This healthy life that started after the divorce was no match for the round of punches that began with the divorce. The last dog of the four I had brought with me from Puerto Rico died. Then Willow, my favorite horse and life mentor, died too. I still feel his loss very deeply. Right after Willow left, my mom began a lengthy decline and died two years later. Her sickness and death were very hard on me. The combined weight of all of these losses injured my heart, and left me emotionally drained. It landed me in a depth of despair. Mom and I had become so close that I just couldn't imagine not having her in my life.

The deep despair left my wounded heart open to making some bad choices. I became involved in several brief relationships that brought on feelings that resonated with that little girl who survived the abuse. This time there was no pull of alcohol or pot. Food became the way I pushed the feelings down. I slowly lost interest in caring for myself with good food, or in the type of exercise that fed me with the endorphins that would leave me feeling good inside. I got sucked into all those same feelings of self-hatred, like the ones I had stored after the abuse.

I needed to start from the beginning. I needed to find the self-respect that would allow me to find value within myself. I renewed my spiritual efforts. More meditation, both longer and more often, became essential. I began to look again for what sparked my innate enthusiasm. What made my heart sing?

Animals! It was time to bring an animal into my life again. I hadn't had an animal since losing my dog and horse. Since before my mom died. I began the search for a good dog.

I found Clyde with the help of a friend who walks dogs at the shelter. He started the process of opening my heart again. I love taking long walks with him. We explored various trails and enjoyed nature together. Six months later, word came that Bonnie, his sister, had been returned to the shelter. It was the third time she had been brought back! She was on the list to be euthanized if she was returned again. Clyde was such a good dog, we couldn't let that happen. I had an animal psychic talk to Clyde about bringing her home. He had some parameters, but agreed. We went to visit her at the shelter, and they recognized each other and wanted to play. That was it! We brought Bonnie home. Now I have two babies. I love them dearly, and having them has been the impetus to get the love moving inside me again. Slowly, bit by bit – but moving.

I started to face my demons. Food, money and those lurking dark thoughts. The hurt and the terror that now had no name. Time to face what was inside. Afraid of what might be revealed. What might arise from within that could not be controlled. How was I ever going to find help with this journey? Could I ever allow there to be help with this journey? I had sunk so low into the disrespect and devaluing myself that I couldn't see the way out. How to arise from this muck?

My body had helped me in the past. Now was the time to listen to it again. Finding the right person to work with, first to open the body. To allow it to speak to me inside my own head.

Not complaining to others but to hear, really hear my deepest fears and feelings. I wanted to hear what was within me. Finding that desire to live and the desire to arise from the depths.

What I needed was a renewed dedication to feel. Feel the feelings. Feel the body. Feel my life. I found a wonderful somatic therapist to guide the journey, and writing my story became a part of my healing.

To this day I am working with these feelings. Finding the way to truly heal the depth of them, and not just cover them up with overachievement and overactivity. I find that the best medicine is to feel the feelings. Go to the inner child, and let her talk. Many people focus on talking to or "at" the inner being. We need to learn to let that inner voice speak its truth. When I go to her and let her speak, I feel light and happy. Writing gets me there, letting her tell her story. Meditation and teaching, working with others who want to go to the depths of their healing. All these ways of expressing my inner self allow me to be in the present and to love who I am.

CHAPTER 10

Understanding and Acceptance

"The first step towards change is awareness.
The second is acceptance."
— NATHANIEL BRANDEN

Following is my journal after a breath-work session:
The breath led me deeper and deeper... All at once I was a newborn infant. Lying flat on a table, no controlled conscious movement possible. I was looking into the eyes of my parents. I recognized them. The awareness of the energy passing between us was so amazing. It was the most prominent feature of the scene. The love flowing between us – through our eyes really. A strong flow: they to me, me to them. There was a color of purplish red with a tinge of blue... I call it love now, but then it was just a sense exchange, of sharing a strong connection of mutual regard. I reveled in it and grew strong and was a part of a whole. A very satisfying, positive feeling.

They moved from my vision as they left the room, and I was still looking straight ahead, just Being. A state I would love to be able to get to now! Then, all at once, there was an intense, unfamiliar sensation! It was on my right side where my neck meets my shoulder. It was sharp and red hot! I didn't know what it was, but now I would call it intense pain. Then he moved into my sightline. I saw him clearly; now I know him. In that instant, as an infant, I recognized him as my arch nemesis of many lifetimes. In an instant, in the dream, I knew we had killed each other many times. A sense of a medieval time, when we were some type of wizards and we had used physical and magical means to fight and eventually destroy one another. In our last life, I had killed him. This time I knew he was in the power position, and he was going to hurt me, to torture me – but he would not kill me. It was a swirling core of memory, visions of lives past. Our hatred of one another and our being bound together to complete some part of this cycle. The revelation allowed me to understand our present life in a way I had been unable to. Rather than see and feel the limited perspective of one life, I could understand his actions with me in a new light. I had been stuck for these last years since remembering the abuse in "Why would he want to hurt me?" "How could he have done these things to me?" "What had I done to deserve this treatment from him?" Now I knew why and what. Now I could forgive him on a level that had been impossible in the past. I could let go of my fear of him as a person now. I am finally free of him. Now to work with the roots within my own being. The ways I had internalized the abuse. The ways I was abusing myself now. Time to work with my own way of being within myself. Then to look at my interactions with others. My relationships with others in this world. How to expand the ego through the propelled heart.

Forgiveness for the abuser has come. I have given him and his hatred to God and Guru. That part is over for me now. At least at this time, I believe so.

The result of this session left me with a new acceptance of what had happened in my early youth. It has been years since this session, and still the acceptance stays with me. Sometimes anger comes up about my difficulties in relationships. Yet, it is mine to work through. There is no longer a need to push against the abusers in my heart. They made their choices, and now I am free to make mine.

I remember a Rubenfeld Synergy session in the office from many years ago (before my own breath-work session that I mentioned above), where a man, abused by a family member at an early age, was at an impasse. He was in deep despair and not understanding what had happened to him. Why the person had done what they had done to him. He stated that he wanted it to be okay. It struck a chord in me. "What that person did to you will never be "okay." They never should have done to you what they did. And, YOU can be okay. You can be okay now, with yourself and your life." So many times, when the wisdom of the ages comes out of my mouth, it is for the client – and it is for me as well. We can be "okay" now. More than okay, we can thrive in our lives now. There is a difference between understanding what someone else chooses to do, and what we can accept and move with now. Between building the life we want to live, and healing those parts of our hearts that were injured by the unconscious acts of others.

CHAPTER 11

Inner Wisdom – The Final Frontier

"There is a universal, intelligent, life force
that exists within everyone and everything."
— Shakti Gawain

Self discovery during and since the Rubenfeld Training has been a true gift. Though the process I discovered myself, and my way of adapting and surviving in the world. One of the tendencies I developed in my life was to change myself to meet the other. This started no doubt with the abuse, as I had been made to serve another's needs and subvert my own wishes. Our experiences in early life become a part of our psyche in such a way as to become a part of who we are. How we are in the world. There is no question, no decision; it is just the way we are. That starts our wondering about the way things are, and if they could be different. About examining the circumstances of life, and the responses that this ego has to them. It is the propelled heart that starts to ask questions.

Changing oneself to meet the other, being able to morph oneself, can be a gift, if I can become the person they need. The person they need as a practitioner and teacher for their healing. In this way, there can be a service to their healing. I became aware that my clients and my friends thought that I thought and felt the same way they did. Did I even know what I thought, independent of their influence? Did I know what I liked and disliked? Not really! That was a shock. How had I lived all these years, having such a strong, determined personality, without being able to know and share what my feelings and deepest thoughts were? The abuse had taught me to keep my deepest needs and feelings to myself. The Air Force experience also helped me learn to become what fit with others, so I could get along. This allowed me to be what people wanted me to be. I fit very well.

One of my mentors in the Rubenfeld Community asked me once, "How do you get people to put you up on a pedestal?" After much consideration, I realized that my expertise in getting along came from my ability to agree and not rock the boat. To show my proficiency in Chiropractic, to solve their problems for them, and to be amicable and to be similar enough to the client so they would be comfortable with me. In this way, they put me on a pedestal. What a long way down when they realized I was not the perfect person I had displayed for their benefit! My years of sitting with this issue, and traveling the road to my own personal healing, have led me to see this morphing as a gift. Not to become what they want me to be, but to become what they need in order for me to be a catalyst for their healing. Never to lose sight of my true self in this equation, but to use "matching" as a tool.

The greatest gift from Spirit or Creator, God or Goddess, is the ability to tap into Source: the inner knowing that is possible through intuition. We all have intuition, and we can learn to develop it. Each of us has the innate ability to tap into that intelligent life force, for it lives within each and every one of us, and in all things.

Some of us experience the inner knowing as a feeling. It may be in the heart, or the gut, or some other part of our body. Since the living intelligence is in all cells, the site of knowing may change in different circumstances and under varying conditions. The knowing may be more visual, or it may come as words. Our mission is to pay attention. In paying attention we can learn to better interpret the messages we are receiving at all times. Our body is the conduit, as are our mind and heart.

I began to listen with an intense interest all those years ago, after not heeding the warnings I received within. The warnings, for example, about the patient in Puerto Rico, whose lung cancer had metastasized to the bones of his spine. I have spent years in meditation, and taking various trainings. Teaching, listening and working with others. That inner life force, that inner voice is friend and guide. Listening to it, not talking at it, is key to our healing. We will look at some exercises in Part II of this book.

CHAPTER 12

A Message from the Red Cloud

"If you want a love message to be heard,
it has got to be sent out.
To keep a lamp burning,
we have to keep putting oil in it."
— MOTHER TERESA

The following conversation took place during one of the writing sessions when going into the "Author Within" state (an altered state connecting to the right brain) to write this book. When I read it I thought of not including it, and then felt I needed to include it after all. This Red Cloud, this Spirit is in all of us and all of creation. Let it speak to you!

"Listen to me now. Do you hear me? I speak to you of the ages. Yes, there have been many lives. There have been many experiences, of which I can tell you all. But, the essence, the true essence is that of love," The Red Cloud said. "You've been wondering about me for years. When the song "Divine Gypsy" says: "I'll sing to my red cloud…" this is me. I am the essence of life: I am The Red Cloud."

"You must know me. Know me now. Know me so you can share me with others. Share how to contact me. The love that is within all creation. This is the essence of all healing. Removal of all physical, mental, emotional, spiritual ailments. This is what throbs and vibrates in the flesh you touch. This is what vibrates within the heart. This is what comes to you in dreams. This is how you learn. Following the course of the nerves in healing others is well and good, but it is not the essence. It is all that flows over the nerves that is important. The life force. This is the essence that is within me, and that you are made of."

"I am the one who lives within you. I have lived within you for a hundred million years. I am your soul essence. I have seen all your egos come and go through the one ego/soul bond. The ego that is bound. Come, listen to me. I have come to free you from the slavery you have been bound in. I have come to free you from this ego that is called some human name. I am the Red Cloud. I am the one to whom you have sung over the centuries. The Red Cloud is me. I have come. Stay with me now. Listen to my words to you. Stand up. Stand in your power. Refuse to allow emotional feelings to overcome you. Emotional feelings that make you an addict to the senses in this and many other lives. You must stand on them. Feel and release. Feel and release the feelings. Do you feel them in your chest as a heaviness? In your body as a pain? Do you feel them in your throat right now as emotional tension? The hot flash that brings the heat through your body?"

"Listen to me. Release them now. Release the pain or the idea of pain from your body, from your life. Listen to me. I am the Red Cloud that lives in you. I am wisdom incarnate. Red because I have fire. I am the reflected fire in the cloud. This is why the cloud is red. The hundred million years we have been together is the blink of an eye."

"Listen to me. This is who you really are. You speak of the love. I am the love. The love that animates you and your heart. Now and forever. Many hearts we have had. Many hearts we have waited. Now is the time for this heart to live and to share. To love and be loved. Not in the limited belief of one relationship, but the entirety of all mankind and all creation. We are the love that lives in all beings. Sing from your heart, from the foundation of your soul. From your body's depths. Listen to me. Write what I tell you now. I am the love. When the Guru says you are loved, he means by me. I am God. The God that lives in you and all creation. This is the love you've wanted all your life. The love you've searched for has been within you all this time. This is the love that animates all things. This is the love that is the magnet that brings you to me. Me to you.

"I am the Red Cloud. Do you see me? Do you feel me? I am within your heart and your chest and in your animals. All the animals' little hearts beat with my love. My essence. I am in all your relations. This is the love of the ages. There is nothing casual about this love. It is the pure essence of the universe. The Higgs Boson particle. The particle that has been discovered holding the universe together. This is the love. This is me. I live in you."

"You must go back to the source, the Red Cloud. The essence not only of creation, but of Spirit. The un-manifested, whence all emerges. This is a spiritual lesson you must get so you can teach others. Let me come through you now. You are loved. You are love. You are love. Love-Attraction that pulls the essence – the Essence of the Red Cloud."

"Is this where we come from?" I ask.

"Yes!" is the reply. "When you touch, there is a vibration. Look at your own arm. Use your will to send more of the Red Cloud of Spirit into it. You can drain it through misuse, so that the Spirit is withdrawn – no essence. That body part will become shriveled. The way you have seen the spine sometimes. With several meditation sessions and practice you can plump up any body part with life and Spirit. Now, right now, send my red essence down your arm. Can you feel it?"

"Yes!" I exclaim.

"See it travel from the medulla oblongata in your brain (the main entrance of life force into the body) to your arm. Red, Red, Red. Blood, life force, heart life force. Flowing down the arm to your fingertips. Allow the healing life force. Allow the embrace of life. Become "thou art that." Where is the resistance now? Allow the contact with life."

"That's it. Breathe and breathe. Let me into you. Hear my words. Let me in. The message I have for you is beyond your ability to understand from your regular mind. Let your mind shut off and let your hand be aroused by me. By me and my essence and energy. Are you ready?"

"Yes! Come into me…" I reply.

"You are the love that holds all things together. It is a lack of love that hurts, and the longer the love is lacking in a tissue, the more it hurts, and then withers and dies. The more sick it becomes. You must work with the energy. The energy in the chakras is love. The energy creates the body." The Red Cloud continued.

"So, it was the energy of my not feeling my own value, the thought of my not having value, that led to the lack of energy. This led to my letting myself be used. I had believed that my only value was in what I could do to serve others. Then that thought, that energy created the thymus problem. Or, I should say, my thymus became sick in that environment. It could not flourish and be healthy with that kind of thought or energy. I lost all sight of a boundary that defined me as being my own expression of life," I reasoned.

"Is the energy metaphorical or is it literal?" I asked.

"Both," was the reply from Spirit.

"I am the Red Cloud. I will teach you if you will let me. Get out of my way. Let me into your heart and mind. Let me in. Let me flow. The red essence of life. I know all. What do you want to know now?"

"Why me? Why are you talking to me now?" I asked.

"You have been developing over these years. Developing over the ages into one who can lead."

"Tell me what stops me from sharing more with others?" I ask.

"I'll tell you. You are afraid. You are squished. You've been squished for lifetimes. Get up! Allow expansion! Don't be afraid to love again. Allow the flow through you. You don't harness it. It flows like electricity around a wire, not in it. Let me flow right now into your arm. Stop judging me. Stop not believing in me. Stop with your negative thinking. I am making you right now. Let me in. Let me make you whole. Let me make you what you should be. Let me make you whole. First you, then you can teach others. Facilitate the healing in others. Don't make me find you again. I am here now. Let me live in you."

CHAPTER 13

The Dance of Evolution

"Our greatest human adventure is
the evolution of consciousness.
We are in this life to enlarge the soul,
liberate the spirit, and light up the brain."
— TOM ROBBINS

L ife is a great dance. We dance, we evolve, whether we are realizing it or not. Much of my life was without seeming intention to me. Yet, looking back, it seems life has held an intention for me. It has been said that we have particular experiences in life in order to evoke specific feelings. These feelings allow us a chance to grow and learn. If we don't get the learning, some other experiences happen, to allow us the opportunity to again experience the feelings, many times very similar, though the evolving experience may seem different on the surface.

Repeating patterns are the tap on the shoulder that asks us to look at our reactions to the world. "Here you are, my child. What are your lessons from this experience?" The Cosmic Beloved seems to be forever patient, ever willing to allow us to repeat opportunities, so as to experience and learn.

I am still on my journey, to be sure. Some things have been learned, some still on replay – until the words and music are learned well, and the pieces can be woven into a new score.

In my private practice in Santa Fe, New Mexico, my clients enjoy exploring their world with me. Some are more interested in the physical side of life, of their body and its workings. Some are intrigued by the metaphor the body represents, the story to be told by the body.

The intuitive way I work privately with my clients has evolved over the last thirty years. I combine my extensive experience of working with others with select portions from various trainings, allowing a customized treatment for each individual. An intuitive scan of the body gives insight into the presenting condition on each visit. The subtle, specific touch, "listening" to the personal nuances of the individual, evokes the internal healing capacity of the body. Using the inborn, reflexive systems of the central and peripheral nervous systems, I facilitate the physical body's own natural corrective ability. While working with the physical body, I use speech that evokes the creative and insightful nature of the client, tapping into their all-knowing, intuitive nature. When the body's messages are received by the client, through their own insight into their life, the body makes rapid changes. These changes are from a deep connection of the body, mind, and spirit. When integrated completely, they can lead to permanent transformation.

Teaching groups of people is another passion of mine. The joy of creating a safe space where creativity and self-discovery can occur is priceless. All people can learn to use their intuition to tap into their own inner wisdom. This intuitive insight can be used to guide and heal one's own life, and it can be used in working with others. Having a deeper understanding of how your intuition works, and how to use it, allows us to tap into this living intelligence that resides within us all. Whether in business, bodywork or counseling, our intuition is invaluable to allow personalized treatment of the client.

I invite you to consciously intend to expand your own consciousness, and join me in the second half of this book – where you will find activities for exploring various aspects of your own body and life experience.

PART II

*Impasse
to Insight*

CHAPTER 14

Body Wisdom and Metaphor

"The body always tells the truth."
— ILANA RUBENFELD

The body has an awareness, a wisdom about our lives that is singular. The point of view that the body has of our lives and the way it expresses this "opinion" is unique. The body can only speak through sensation. Somatic (of the body) sensation is a very nuanced language in each individual body. This is due to each person's varied life experiences, and the unique response each individual has to the same stimuli. Each person holds the ultimate source of knowledge in his or her own body. The imperative is to learn how to receive the messages of the body, and then to allow the interpretation to come through our own system, not that of some other person and not through our educated, logical brain.

The physical body is a metaphorical representation of a person's life. The story of one's life can be read through or interpreted by reading the story that the body is telling. The overview the body displays has many clues to follow, and this is sometimes harder for the person to see by him- or herself. The overall posture is a sign. The way each part of the body is held in relation to the other parts. Where the body moves from or how it is organized to move. How the breath moves through the various places in the body. Where one breathes from. The placement of the feet in standing, walking and sitting. All these are signs to be followed. If one jumps to analysis too quickly, many details are missed.

The body is talking to us all the time, if we would but listen. We discover a rich tapestry when we can begin to hear the language of the body's sensations. This wisdom is coming to us in various forms through the body, both physical and emotional or energetic. For what is emotion but energy in motion? The energy moving in the body has a specific physical sensation and corresponding emotion.

The most important source of information about one's own life and healing is contained within the body. What is actually happening in our lives, the lessons to be learned, what needs to heal, what is needed to heal – all this is contained within. Our challenge, for the most part, is learning how to access this information.

Another challenge in our modern culture is that we are encouraged to NOT listen, to obliterate the messages our body is sending us. Whatever the symptom (somatic sensation) the body may present has a corresponding medication that will eliminate the message. "Can't sleep? Take this pill." "That one doesn't work? Try this other one." Drowsy in the morning after that pill? Take this one!" "Having trouble eating the foods that cause your digestive tract distress? We have a pill for that!" "Low-back pain due to overwork, overuse or lack of exercise? Take this pill and put on this muscle liniment, and add this hot or cold pack." It is as if all the ads are telling us: "Please don't try to figure out what is going on!" The true cause of the distress. That would put many, many manufacturers out of business. It is said that if all women learned to love the way they looked and accepted themselves as beautiful and worthy, the entire world economy would collapse due to the fall of the cosmetic and skin care manufacturers, along with other industries that profit from making us look better. **Look** better, not **feel** better about ourselves and our lives.

Our next challenge is actually whether we want to hear the body and know its message. Imagine someone asleep in their bed. A fire begins to engulf the house. Someone comes to the door, banging on it and yelling "Fire, Fire! Get out of the house, now!" No one would want the rescuer to shut up and go away. No way! The disturbed sleeper would jump up and run for dear life. Profusely thanking the rescuer, who gave the early warning, for saving their life. The body is the rescuer, giving early warning that something is amiss. Many people just want the body to stop giving its warning signals. To stop the uncomfortable sensations, so they can go back to sleep. Back to living life in comfortable ignorance of whatever is wrong.

The body, however, will continue trying to deliver the message, even when given some type of masking drug or treatment. The message will move to another area of the body or become so insistent that it cannot be ignored. It is uncommon for the message, the warning, to be only about the body. Usually the message is about something in the person's life that's affecting him or her, either mentally, emotionally or spiritually. The body will continue to present the warning in various ways until the message is received. Donald Epstein, D.C., founder of Network

Spinal Analysis, said: "We must learn to listen to the body's whispers, so we don't have to endure its screams." How true! How many times have people come to my office complaining of some physical sensation, and when asked how long the symptom had been present, they reply, "Oh, it only hurt a little bit at first, thirty years ago. Now it is unbearable!"

This is where metaphor comes into play. This was a term and concept I knew absolutely nothing about when I started the Rubenfeld Synergy Training, about eight years into my private chiropractic practice. All I knew was that my patients tended to repeat the same type of injury, or the same symptoms recurred, when similar circumstances came into their lives.

What the heck was a metaphor? Of course, I didn't ask outright at the training. To admit that I didn't know something was something my system abhorred! No way I was going to say that I didn't know something that the others seemed to be comfortable with and knowledgeable about. Now I see metaphor as a representation of something. A metaphor allows you some space to see something from another point of view, or from some distance, so you can gain perspective. My Southern relatives would use metaphor all the time in the way they spoke. "That boy can eat a pie like a hog going after its supper."

The way your body feels physically is a clue to what is happening in your life. The metaphor is an analogy your body has created for your life. A simple example: let's say your knee has a pain. When you tune into that pain, you describe it as pinching. Staying with the pinching long enough to allow the experience of the physical sensation to sink into your neurological system, you may begin to notice images or words or emotions as they enter your awareness. As you follow this trail, you may be reminded of a past or present situation in your life. Ah, you realize how this situation, person, place or thing is somewhat like pinching. Many times, just receiving the message may relieve the symptom of the pinch in your knee. It may seem miraculous, and I have seen it repeated many times with myself and clients. Some people would like to believe that every problem with the knee is "a problem moving forward," as a popular book states. This is a place to start, perhaps, but it is through following the actual physical sensation and staying with it, not removing or relieving it, that will yield the treasure of knowledge that will lead to permanent relief.

I once had a nagging knee pain that was not debilitating, but it just wouldn't let up. I had been wrestling with a decision of whether to go to the Bahamas with a friend to swim with the dolphins. Though I had grown up in Puerto Rico and had seen many dolphins and experienced them swimming near small boats or surfing waves, I had never been on a trip that was dedicated to swimming with and communing with the dolphins. I wanted to go so badly! However, I had just moved to Santa Fe, and the cost of the relocation had been harder on my finances than anticipated. I could not go! I kept coming to the same conclusion again and again. **I can not go!** I was extremely frustrated! Then one day I was driving my car (it was my right knee, the gas leg) and mulling over the predicament. "I want to go! I cannot go!" I wrestled with myself. Then it dawned on me that I could go. I could put it all on credit cards and just pay them later. That is what credit cards are for, right? However, I was CHOOSING not to go because it was not a wise financial decision at that time. I was choosing, instead of being stuck in "I cannot go." My knee was instantly relieved, and I have not had pain in it since. I never received treatment for that problem. That was twelve years ago. The "cannot go" place in my mind was stuck in my knee. When I looked at it from a different perspective, I was released from the discomfort.

Granted, there are times when treatment is vitally necessary. Receiving the body's messages, however, will always assist in the healing of any injury or illness in the body. The body always has messages for us in the sensations it is experiencing – especially with organ disease, which we will look at later. It is important in seeking healing for the body that we also receive the message the body is sending, so that it does not have to repeat the same sensations or illness or injury to try once again to send its intelligence to our awareness.

EXERCISE

Getting to Know Breath
(inspired by Stage 1 of *The 12 Stages of Healing*
by Donald Epstein)

This is a way to deepen your relationship with your body: the first step in learning to observe and listen to your body without judgment or expectations. The value here is the foundation you will lay for being able to tune into yourself and your needs and desires. There are necessary necessities, those that we need to survive and thrive, and there are unnecessary necessities, the things we may want to indulge in, but that aren't important for our health and wellness. Being able to distinguish between these is vital. We can save ourselves a lot of trouble by being able to tell the difference. Our body knows immediately, and it will share this knowledge with us if we will but ask, and then listen to the response. Being able to quiet your mind and listen to your body is essential. This exercise lets you start the process by making things simple and easy. It is the foundation for all the other exercises to follow.

Extended Directions

Allow yourself to sit (sit in a firm, straight chair with feet on the floor), or lie comfortably on your back, with your knees bent up and your feet on the floor.

Become aware of your breathing. Place your hands on your lower rounded belly, and breathe, under your hands, so that your hands move up and down. What is this like for you? Is it hard or easy? Stay with this for several minutes. Notice any emotion that may or may not arise. Stay with it, without changing it, without fixing it. Allow yourself to just notice. Let this all go.

Now, move your hands to where your ribs end. Breathe into this place, under your hands, so that your hands move up and down. Continue for several minutes, noticing what this is like for you. Is it easier or harder than the first place? Notice any feelings that arise as you do this. Again, stay with what arises from within you. No need to change it or fix it.

Now, move your hands up to your chest. Breathe, again, under your hands, so that your hands move up and down. Continue for several minutes. What is breathing into this place like? Easiest, hardest or in between the effort made in the other two places?

Notice any emotions that may be associated with breathing into this place. Stay with it long enough to become familiar with your sensations, whatever they might be.

Now, go back to the easiest place. Let everything else go and breathe into this place, whichever of the three it might be. Allow yourself to continue breathing so that your hands move up and down with the movement of the breath in your body. Stay with this place only, for the next five minutes. Allow any feelings, memories, thoughts to emerge from this place, and just let them flow through. No thinking about them in the sense of trying to figure out what they mean or where they come from. Just allow the flow. Notice what your body's way of talking to you from this aspect is. Is it more visual, auditory, or feeling? You are learning to listen, not interpret. After the exercise, allow yourself a few minutes to write any impressions or draw any images that will allow you to deepen your experience of this exercise.

Diamond Point Directions

◆ Assume a comfortable position lying on the back, knees bent up.
◆ Become aware of the breath.
◆ Place hands on lower belly by hips; breathe so hands rise and fall with belly movement.
◆ Be aware of what this is like for you.
◆ Place hands on upper belly where ribs end; breathe so hands rise and fall.
◆ Be aware of what happens for you.
◆ Place hands on upper chest; breathe so hands rise and fall.
◆ Be aware of what is happening within you.
◆ Go back to the easiest place to feel the hands move up and down with breath.
◆ Stay with hands here; breathe into this place for five minutes.
◆ Notice feelings, images, memories, allowing them to flow through, without thinking or figuring out.
◆ Write or draw anything that allows you to express your experience.

Awareness is the first step in the healing process. When the body is displaying some symptom, it has a message. The body will continue to display the symptom until the message is received. If the symptom is removed through any means of treatment, without the message being received, the pain or sensation may just move to another location. It is important to try to hear the message, to receive it. Most people, when asked to talk to their body, find it strange. Then they will say something like, "Stop it!" or "Cut it out, settle down!" This is not effective. When we pay attention to the actual physical sensation, it may not change at all, or it may tighten and worsen. Imagine you are hurting, and someone comes over and says, "Stop it!" How would you feel? You might get angry or sad. It certainly wouldn't help you with your pain. Telling the body, "You're okay," or "It will be all right," usually won't help either, because if these were true for the body, there would be no recurring sensation.

The directions that follow will have you become very observant of the area of your body that is displaying a symptom. Choose one specific place, so you can pay close attention. Stay in the observation mode so as not to disrupt the experience with trying to figure it out. There will be plenty of time for that later. The instructions will walk you through visual, kinesthetic, auditory, gustatory (taste) and olfactory (smell) cues to define precisely what is happening in the area. This also takes you deeper into your experience and actually changes your brain-wave state to alpha waves (or deeper), to allow for a state of increased creativity and insight. This is in contrast to our usual beta-wave state of waking when we are analyzing and figuring, complaining and problem solving. For these exercises, we want to be observant and open to whatever wants to emerge from within.

Once you have observed and have a good sense of this place, begin a dialogue. Something that includes what you have observed will be helpful. Such as: "I know you are hurting now." Or "I feel your pain." A statement that acknowledges the place, and what you have observed. "I see that you are holding what looks like a dark-green, triangular object within your tissue": whatever you have seen, heard, felt, smelled or tasted.

Be patient with yourself as you begin to explore this way of being with your body. You probably aren't used to gathering such detailed information from your body. We have been trained to NOT pay attention to the body's cues – and now you are learning to slow down and take in ALL the cues of your body.

Notice what happens to the area with your being so attentive to it. Many times, just recognizing it – acknowledging the sensation – will allow for some positive change. We all like to be heard or seen, don't we? The body is the same. In fact, the body can be likened to a young child. It will speak in simple terms, with short, simple words and sentences. Usually five words or less. It likes to be talked to in the same way. If you hear long orations when you ask for responses, it is your logical left brain taking over. Also, you will confuse the body (right brain) with long orations and paragraphs that cloud the issue. Be concise, and get to the point in as few words as possible.

Beginning the dialogue by talking to the place is usually helpful in the next step, asking the place to talk to you. To deliver the message it is holding for you. Here it is important to not elicit a defensive response by asking "why" questions. Imagine when someone comes up to you and asks, "Why are you doing x, y and z?" This puts you into having to defend your choices. If they are really concerned for your welfare they may ask "I notice you're doing x, y and z, and I am wondering what is happening with you." Wouldn't you respond to that type of question in a more neutral way, and be more willing to share?

Verbal and auditory people tend to have an easier time with conversation, per se, once they can slow it down to having a simple dialog with few words and short sentences. Visual people may have a conversation with images. They may change the image and see how the body responds in kind, or the image may change with verbal questions and comments. Kinesthetic or touch people may have all the conversation in sensations. Emotional people may sense the shifting in their emotions as the dialog progresses. This is really about learning the language of your body. We are all unique. Be patient and allow your body to reveal itself to your mind. Learning, accepting and appreciating our body's unique mode of communication is priceless.

EXERCISE

Discover the Message of a Physical Symptom

Extended Directions

Sit in a firm chair with your feet on the floor, or lie on your back with your arms by your side. Become aware of your breath. Stay with the breath for several rounds of inhalation and exhalation. Become aware of the contact that your body is making with the chair or floor. Notice the way your body allows the support of the chair or floor. If you are lying on the floor, while leaving your head in the same spot on the floor, gently roll your head from side to side by tracing a line in the air with your nose. Notice the movement that is possible. Is the movement between the two sides equal? Is it easier to one side than another? How far down the spine can you feel the movement? No control: just watch, feel, and listen within.

By noticing yourself before you start any exercise, you allow yourself to become aware of any changes that occur through performing the exercise and your awareness efforts.

Once your mind is quiet, allow yourself to identify the area that has the pain or specific symptom. If the place wanting your attention is not readily apparent, scan the body by starting at the head and noticing the parts of your body from head to toe. Allow the place wanting your attention to emerge: you will know when you come to it. It will be different in feeling, or the way it seems to you in your mind's eye. No judgment or complaint. Allow yourself to go into the depth of the sensation. What does it feel like to you in this moment? Breathe into it. Allow it to reveal itself in all its dimensions to you. As you go deeper into the sensation, you may find other sensations. Stay with it. Is there any emotion? If so, don't analyze, just observe. How does that emotion express itself in this place? Is any other place in your body affected?

Is there any color or shape? How big is it? Perhaps there is an image that is new to you, or a memory. Just allow yourself to experience whatever you see or feel without judging it or figuring it out. Stay with observing it at this point.

Notice if there are any sounds associated with your experience. Any smells? You are collecting information of the type that your five senses collect. Sight, sound, smell, taste and touch. We are adding kinesthetic or physical sensation to this list, as that is the manifestation of the touch sense. Does what you are experiencing through these senses remind you of anything or anyone? Any specific time in your life? Is there a particular memory associated with this area of the body where you are experiencing physical pain or a symptom?

Now that you have used the five common senses to deepen your contact with the place, we will move into using the sixth sense: intuition. We all have intuition, and there are exercises to develop it further. The following are ways to deepen your practice of using and developing your intuition. Becoming aware of these subtle somatic sensations is a form of intuitive experience.

Notice and follow the lead of whatever you are finding interesting, or whatever is standing out in your awareness of this place. Stay with it. Continue to feel and sense all that you are aware of.

Notice what is happening in the area now that you have become keenly aware of it.

Once you have established a relationship with this part of you and have sensed some kind of response to your messages, the next step is to have a conversation with the place. Allow any question or curiosity you may have to arise naturally and easily. As the conversation progresses, the place may have questions for you. The conversation can progress as if you were talking to some other person.

At the end of your time with your body, allow yourself to again become aware of the contact you are making with the chair or floor. Has it changed in any way? Is your body more willing and/or able to receive the support of the chair or floor? If you are lying on the floor, roll your head from side to side again, as you did in the beginning of the exercise, by tracing a line in the air with your nose. Notice what has changed from the first time. Is it easier or harder? Is there more or less equal movement from side to side? Do you experience more movement down your spine than you did originally, or not? Note anything that comes into your awareness. You may want to keep a journal of your experiences with yourself: an "Awareness Journal."

Diamond Point Directions

◆ Sit or lie comfortably.

◆ Become aware of your breath for several minutes.

◆ Become aware of your body, in contact with the surface you are lying or sitting on.

◆ Notice your weight and posture.

◆ If you are lying down, roll your head from side to side and take note of movement.

◆ Scan your body and identify a place that wants your attention right now.

◆ Breathe into that place and notice sensations present.

◆ Identify all sensations: what it looks like, feels like, sounds like, smells and tastes like.

◆ Just observe. Don't analyze or judge.

◆ Stay with what is interesting to you.

◆ Notice memories that arise, if any.

◆ Speak to the place, acknowledge what it has revealed to you in a brief sentence. IE "I know your tired."

◆ Allow any answers from the area to arise through words or changes in the above sensations.

◆ Continue the conversation, as if with another person; keep it short and simple.

◆ Become aware again of where you are sitting or lying, and breathe.

◆ Roll the head from side to side.

◆ Keep an Awareness Journal by writing or drawing an expression of your experience.

One must become aware that something is not working, or that something is not quite right with the body or in one's life. There may be a physical symptom in the body, or an outward symptom of unrest in the home, family, relationship, or workplace. There may be some recurring emotion, with or without apparent reason. There may be an emotion related to a particular area of the body, or with a particular symptom. Another important, yet often overlooked possibility is a recurring situation. There may be a theme of "the horrible boss" or "betrayal" or "abandonment" that keeps repeating in one's life, in various scenarios. The first step is the awareness that is growing within you.

Many times we experience the same emotion in different situations. Or, the same emotions arise with specific situations. These emotions can be quite strong and overwhelming. They may come on with speed and by surprise. All at once, there you are, angry, sad, or scared, without any warning. Trying to go into the emotion may, at first, seem to stop it. Try to pay attention quickly to avoid losing it. You may already have become aware that you have recurring emotions.

Some people actually get the feeling of falling out of their heads, and they need to pinch themselves or squeeze something to get back into their bodies. This is a sign of mild dissociation, and it is evidence of a severe trauma in the past. Should this happen to you, please seek professional help in exploring these issues.

Once you decide to work with your recurring emotional responses to life, we will proceed with an exercise similar to listening to a recurring physical sensation. We always need to remember to say things that will build our relationship with our body. "I know you are scared now." "I understand that you are angry.""I recognize that you are sad now." We must do this, rather than make statements that deny the sensations and emotions, such as "Stop that now!" or "Just take it easy now!" or "Get over it!" Commands are generally not helpful. Remember how you respond in your everyday life to commands. Most people feel resistance to commands.

With questions and comments, it is usually more effective to keep things general, which allows more information to come in. When you already know (or think you do), it stifles any new information.

Always stop when you need to. If the feelings or sensations become too intense, stop your inquiry and become aware of your feet. Place them on the floor, if they are not already there. Breathe deeply into your feet, in through your feet, as if you had nostrils on the bottom of your feet. Then breathe out through your feet, through those nostrils on the bottom of your feet, into the earth. Continue this deep breathing – into the ground and in from the ground – until you feel calm and grounded. Then walk around slowly and deliberately, aware of your feet at all times. If you find that the feelings are intense, or if you already know that you have intense emotions that can be overwhelming, seek professional help before starting with this inquiry. A therapist who works in a somatic way can be very effective in clearing unwanted recurring emotions, for example, a Rubenfeld Synergist, Somatic Experiencing practitioner or Hakomi Integrated practitioner. Many therapists today use a somatic approach and would be able to explain their approach more fully in a consultation. These exercises are meant to be an introduction to accessing and working with these intense emotions. It is always easier, and usually quicker in coming to some resolution, when working with a qualified professional. I always make this suggestion when working with emotions, especially because they are so powerful when experienced fully in the body.

EXERCISE

Discover the Message of a Recurring Emotion

Extended directions

Wherever you are, the emotion you recognize occurs. Stop, and notice how your body responds to this emotion. What do you actually feel physically with this emotion? How is your breathing? Deep, shallow, fast, slow. Where is your breathing? Upper chest, mid-chest, lower belly. What muscles are tight? Neck, back, hips, legs, arms, feet. Are there any loose muscles? Where? Are you "in your body" (experiencing it easily) or "out of your body" (in your head and not feeling your body)? Where is this emotion based in your body? Ask and allow yourself to know. Place a hand on that place in your body, if you can reach it. If not, hold the place in your mind's eye. What does it feel like, physically, right there? Describe this in as much detail as possible. Breathe into it. Is there a color, shape, sound, smell or taste associated with this emotion in this place? By what or by whom was this emotion triggered? What was happening when it got triggered? What were the exact words or situation that triggered the emotion? Does this remind you of anything or anyone?

What is happening with the emotion as you listen in this way? What is your physical body's response? Continue to breathe into the place, and notice any transformation. If you are still able to continue, do you have any message you'd like to send to this place? To this feeling?

Once you feel there is a relationship of some kind with the area or the emotion, you might ask a question like: "Is there anything that you want me to know now?" "Is there something that you need now?"

Always stop when you need to. Become aware of your feet. Place them on the floor. Breathe deeply into your feet, in through your feet, as if you had nostrils on the bottom of your feet. Then breathe out through your feet, through those nostrils on the bottom or your feet, into the earth. Continue this deep breathing into the ground, and in from the ground, until you feel calm and grounded. Then walk around slowly and deliberately, aware of your feet at all times. Seek professional help if you feel overwhelmed.

Diamond Point Directions

◆ Start when the emotion occurs, or call it forth by recalling what brings it on.

◆ Notice your breathing: rate, rhythm, location.

◆ Notice what happens in your body physically: muscle tension, pain, ache.

◆ Notice if you are "in" the experience or "observing" it.

◆ Notice where the emotion is located in your body.

◆ Place your hand on the physical location of the emotion.

◆ If you can't reach the place, hold it in your mind's eye.

◆ What is that specific place like: what do you see, feel, hear, smell or taste.

◆ What situation, words or other stimulus provoke this reaction: what makes it worse.

◆ Who, what, when, or where does it remind you of?.

◆ What happens to the emotion when you pay attention?

◆ What happens in your body when you pay attention?

◆ What is happening with your breath?

◆ What message do you want to send to this place/to this feeling in you?

◆ If relationship is established, ask for a message.

◆ **Stop and seek professional guidance if you feel overwhelmed.**

CHAPTER 15

The Inner Wisdom of Dis-Ease

The body no longer appears as a sick or irrational demon,
but as a process with its own inner logic and wisdom."
— George MacDonald

O rgans and their functions are metaphorical messages about our lives: clues to the way we live our lives in the world. We usually become interested in some specific organ when there is a problem. We have been told by a practitioner that some symptom or illness is caused by a particular organ. The first step is to research the normal function of that organ. There are books, some for the professional, some for the layman, which can be consulted to ascertain the normal function of a healthy organ. The simplest and briefest explanation will supply sufficient information to begin your exploration of the metaphoric implications.

Let's look at an example. One summer, my nephew was visiting from Oregon and he wanted to go white-water rafting. What a wonderful idea! There are many white-water rafting companies in Santa Fe, and we researched and chose a reputable company that promised high adventure along the Rio Grande, including traveling through the Taos Box. This particular section of river narrows, and allows for some real white-water action. We made the trip and it was so much fun! The day was warm, and there was a lot of sun. On our return, we all retired to our rooms for a little nap before dinner. While trying to drift off, my heart began to beat like a drum; it was as if I'd been running a foot race. What was going on?! My resting heart rate was 120 beats a minute. This is not normal! The resting heart rate of a non-athlete is commonly around 80 beats a minute. No matter how I tried to relax, to breathe deeply, to meditate, nothing slowed my heart down. After about an hour, it did calm down.

In the following weeks, the same type of episode repeated. I would be reading or resting, and my heart rate would jump up to 120-plus beats a minute. My medical doctor told me I was experiencing hyperthyroidism, an increased function of the thyroid gland. This is much less common than hypothyroidism, a decreased function of the thyroid gland. I tried the medication, which lowered my immune function. I also had to take beta-blockers to slow my heart down and lower my blood pressure. I was miserable. After refusing to use even aspirin for most of my life, now it seemed that my life depended on taking several strong medications.

Deciding to try a natural remedy, I went to a well-known doctor who used supplements. She determined which supplements were lacking, and what dosage I needed, by muscle testing. She also wrongly began to lower my medications using muscle testing. I ended up in the emergency room with a thyroid storm! This is when the thyroid, which regulates metabolism, goes haywire and signals all the organs to go into hyperdrive. They admitted me to the emergency room with blood pressure of 190/130 (normal

120/80) and a pulse rate of 170 (remember: normal would be 80)! It took eight hours to calm things down and for them to release me. The doctor was adamant as he told me: "You must choose. Are you going to live without that thyroid or die with it? At your age (forty-two), you are ripe for a heart attack! And after tonight, the likelihood of one coming on you fairly soon is great!"

The choices were to have surgery to remove my thyroid gland (I am deathly afraid of surgery) or have thyroid ablation therapy. I decided to receive thyroid ablation, which is where they give you iodine laced with radiation to kill the thyroid gland. Iodine is specifically absorbed by the thyroid, so the radiation concentrates there and kills it. This was a horrific experience for someone who had not taken so much as an aspirin since childhood. I was glowing for three days, during which time the instructions were to stay at least three feet from all other living beings – husband, dogs and plants included!

After the "treatment," things were still not right. I finally found some bodyworkers who used hands-on therapy for treating the organs. When they did the initial assessment, they found that it was my thymus that was the problem, not the thyroid. They found my thymus to be toxic, and that this toxicity had been irritating my thyroid. Research verified that all blood supply to and from the thymus went directly through the thyroid. No wonder I still felt something was wrong. In a general physiology book, the function of the thymus was explained as being the gland in the body that told all the cells "who is the 'I'." The thymus is very large at birth, and all immune cells pass through it to be marked as to who or what is the individual being. This allows the immune system to identify an invader, "something that is not me."

Wow! This was a breakthrough for me. I recognized that my way of moving in the world had been to confuse my boundaries. I would not recognize myself as the vital subject to be protected at all costs. "Other" was so important to me that I would consider the other's welfare of higher priority than my own welfare. I realized immediately that the first "treatment" I should have demanded was a divorce from the man who was driving me crazy. Yet I had put his health and welfare before my own, and I was sacrificing my sanity and dignity to stay with him. To stay because of the vow, "in sickness and in health till death do us part." I had almost died to keep my vows!

The exercise below will allow you to gain insight into the messages your organ(s) may be trying to give you about your life and the way you are living it. Keep judgment out of the way and you can garner information that will allow you to take a more active role in your healing process. This will not replace medical treatment by any means, but it will assist in getting your body on your side, by getting your heart, mind and emotions in alignment with your health goals.

EXERCISE

Organ Dis-Ease or System Dysfunction as Metaphor

Once you have a diagnosis of a particular malfunction or disease of an organ or system of the body, do some research into the exact function of that organ or part of the body. Locate a simple explanation in a layman's guide to normal human physiology. Then find the simple explanation of what is not working properly. State the normal function and the abnormal function in as few words as possible. Make simple statements so you can hear and feel the obvious. After you've finished the research, and you have made the concise statements; sit, breathe, meditate. Allow time for insight from your intuitive nature. Allow the link to emerge between what the organ should be doing and what is going wrong. Then allow the insight into your life to emerge. What is not working? How does your way of behaving or functioning in the world mimic or compare to what is happening in that organ? These are your clues to what needs to change in your life so that the organ can fully recover and heal. All of it is right there, in the flesh! Remember, you may still need Western-medicine intervention to stop the disease process. Consult your physician.

Diamond Point Directions

◆ Research a simple explanation of the normal function of your problem organ or body system.
◆ Research a simple explanation of the malfunction (or diagnosis).
◆ Make concise statements and study them.
◆ Calm your mind through use of breath and/or meditation.
◆ Allow the insight of similarity between your present life and these statements about the body.
◆ Ask yourself what you need to change or address in your life that would address the malfunction.
◆ Draw or write any expression of the insights you have received.

Life situations can often give us insight into our habitual ways of living that are not functional or health-enhancing. Often events, situations or relationships can seem to repeat themselves throughout our lives. These recurrences are clues to issues that need healing within ourselves. These "repeat offenders" are metaphorical of the ways we are interacting with the world around us. It is no coincidence that you fall for the same type of guy (or girl), or that you always have a lousy boss or uncooperative neighbors. When the same types of situations or people surround us, we need to pay attention to the messages the world is trying to deliver. Many times these are the very situations that precede illness. When we ignore the signs that something is unbalanced in our world, disease can follow. The body finally gives in to the pressure of the imbalance, and the way it is causing the body/ mind/spirit/emotions to respond and react to life.

For example, a friend of mine was always meeting men who had issues with keeping a job, wanting a job in the first place, and drinking too much alcohol. They tended to need help coping with life in general. She would take charge and try to make things right for them. Help them with money and ideas. Try to make a solid home life. Then they fought and struggled with issues of her being controlling and him not living up to her expectations. To put things simply: She was being the mother and he the naughty boy. The dynamic kept them in a power struggle. Facing this could have allowed them a variety of options to either resolve the strife or separate.

I remember a time in my life when I thought that everyone felt and thought the same as I did. What a surprise to me in my early twenties to discover that people did not feel and think like me. Others had different priorities, and what was important to me might not be as important to others. What I thought should be done, and the "right way" to do it, was not necessarily the "right way" for others. I had always looked for the "right way," the "one way," that something should be done so I wouldn't make a mistake. Well, lo and behold. There is no one "right way" for anything. Surprise! We must each view life itself, and decide our own priorities. Determine what is the "right way" for us. The key is to understand one's self. To be able to observe the metaphors speaking to us each day in our lives, through our bodies and with all the situations in our life. To heal by knowing and accepting our Self, our own true nature.

Working with these emotions can be intense. Working through them is always easier with an experienced empathetic therapist who is familiar with how the body holds these feelings. Seek the help of a qualified professional. These exercises are meant to be an example of how you can access and discover what is held within you. If you know that you have had intense experiences or extreme reactions in the past, when remembering or working with your emotions, it is probably best to seek out professional help before venturing into any past episode in your life. Be gentle with yourself.

EXERCISE

Words and Situations, Clues to Cause of Imbalance

Extended Directions

Part A: Notice when you are triggered by a situation (the way someone speaks to you, the way you always end up in a certain situation at work or with friends) or by certain words (what the boss, your lover, your friend, your co-worker said). What exactly is the situation (described in as few words as possible, e.g. "I'm always last" or "I am never chosen for those special assignments" or "She or he never notices me" or "She or he never thanks me for the kindness I've shown or what I've done for them")? What exactly are the words ("You're never ready on time" or "I have had enough of your _____")?. Once you've identified the words or situation, allow yourself to sit with this information. Repeat the words or situation in your mind. Feel the feelings that are evoked. What is the emotion? Where is it in your body? Place a hand there if you can. What is happening physically/energetically in that place? Breathe into this place. You may be served by stopping here and repeating this several times before moving on to the next step.

Part B: Imagine a timeline of your life stretching out behind you. Allow yourself to float above it. Allow yourself to go back to the first time you felt this way. The first time those words were spoken to you. The first time you were in that situation. How old are you? What is happening in your life? Where are you? Who is involved? How did you feel then? Breathe. What do you know now that you did not know then? Talk to that "you" of the past and let him/her know what you know now. Allow him/her to respond to you. How do they feel now? If it is appropriate, embrace that "you" of the past. Allow that younger "you" to share whatever he/she would like to. Respond if appropriate and finish the exchange. Thank that part of you for being willing to come forward and share. Allow yourself to come back to this present time. Breathe. Notice how you feel now. What happens when you recall the words or situation that you started this exercise with? How is the place that held the emotional response? Breathe deeply. Feel your feet on the floor. Open your eyes. How does the room look? Stand and feel your feet on the floor. Move, slowly at first, allowing yourself to feel how it is to be you now. What are you aware of now?

Always stop and seek professional help to assist you in processing these emotions if they feel too intense.

Diamond Point Directions

Part A:

◆ Notice what words or situations trigger an intense emotional response from you.

◆ Make a concise statement about the situation.

◆ Breathe deeply and experience your body.

◆ Repeat the words or situation in your mind.

◆ Notice the emotions: where are they in your body, what do they feel like physically?

◆ Breathe into this place; place a hand there if possible.

◆ Stay here, breathe and acknowledge it.

◆ Repeat several times over several days or weeks.

Part B: After working with A several times

◆ Imagine a timeline of your life stretching out behind you.

◆ Ask yourself: When was the first time I heard this phrase or experienced this situation? Float back over line to that time.

◆ How old are you? Where are you? What is happening?

◆ Breathe deeply; slow down.

◆ What do you know now that you didn't know then?

◆ Talk to the past "you" and share the wisdom you have now.

◆ Allow that younger "you" to share whatever he/she would like to.

◆ Breathe deeply; slow down.

◆ Complete the interchange with that younger "you."

◆ Come back to the now. How do you feel now?

◆ What happens when you recall the words or situation now?

◆ Physically describe the place that had been holding the emotion.

◆ Breathe deeply into your feet on the floor.

◆ Move slowly, stay with physical sensations.

◆ Stop when necessary at any point and seek professional help if needed.

CHAPTER 16

Value of Self

"Try not to become a man of success,
but rather try to become a man of value."
— ALBERT EINSTEIN

E quality. That is what is missing. I devalued myself in the past, so I now feel betrayed more easily. Could this play a role for others? De-valuing themselves and seeing others of more value. Then, on feeling this, the theme repeats again and again. What a dynamic! Can this be a key to unraveling the mystery of healing?

When people see themselves as having value, at least the same value as others, then they deserve whatever they need. Others also can be recognized as deserving what they need. There is freedom for all. No bondage. Each is allowed their life experience. When we are of equal value, we meet.

If one perceives him- or herself (or is perceived by others) as of more value, that person usually will take more than his or her share, and the one perceived (by themselves or others) as of lesser value tends to give themselves away. In some relationships, the one who feels of more value will create lesser value in the partner. The one of perceived greater value feels disappointed in the other, and the partner feels unworthy. The unworthy one gives of their essence and the one of perceived greater value takes. With the lesser one feeling worse and worse about himself/herself, the relationship needs to end (as the lesser-value person needs the relief). There is no middle ground to meet on.

This is a very interesting dynamic. To see/think/feel of self and other as having equal value creates a safe and inspired relationship. There can be a meeting of body, mind and soul. A true and full sharing of the essence of the individuals. Mutual healing and growth can occur. The essence of life force is shared. There is more here. When I am of value, I am loved. The other is of value, and he or she is loved. We are both of value and loved. We ARE love. We can help each other to see, to know, to understand. We have to have love and value vibration.

By feeling of value, and being love itself, we find equality. We can feel equal and expect the same from the other. How can each of us help others to know that they are of value? We can treat others as equal with our speech and our attitude toward them. We can treat them in a way that honors their uniqueness, and respect their value in the world. We can expect respect in return from others, and respect ourselves in our ways of behaving in the world. We can love ourselves and each other. Love is vibration. If I am in the love, if I am love, that will bring others and their vibration up to a higher resonance.

How might we do that? Do we find value or make value? No! We each have inherent value. When we allow ideas to flow from the heart, Spirit will show the way.

If we follow the heart path, where does it go? What does it look like? As I look inside myself right now, my heart looks purple – dark purple – and I see lines. Lines of life? Or are the lines the wrinkles of having lived? Or is it aging and death trying to encroach on the heart? How to know? Relax the heart and let blood in. How can we live with value now? What does that mean? It means to value this life. This chance to live and feel.

The value emerges from respect of self. To respect oneself. Respect comes from doing and behaving in the way that we know is from and for our highest good.

I suspect that my mom saw herself as being of less value. She couldn't digest food well most of her life. She suffered with indigestion, and at the end of her life, she could not eat at all. She suffered with recurring pneumonia, and she could not breathe on her own at the end of her life. There was a complete inability to take in nourishment of any kind at the end of her life. Had this resulted from a lack of value?

Value and Love: two great tenets we all need to truly heal our lives. We need value and love to be able to expand our consciousness and thereby evolve. I believe this is a part of what we need to evolve while incarnate in the body. Value is defined as believing that someone or something is important or useful. Acknowledging value leads to respect. This is our next topic, and it is very close to value. They are two sides of the same coin.

Do you recognize your value? Are you able to maintain a recognition of your inherent value over the long term? Are there thoughts that could enable you to hold onto a knowing of that value? Are there ways you could increase your value in your own eyes?

EXERCISE

Self-Value Assessment

Part A: Allow yourself to sit or lie down in a comfortable place. Start, as always, with some nice deep breaths. Take note of your body and any sensations you may be experiencing at this time.

Imagine that you are viewing a movie of your life. You are now the observer, watching in a detached way the actions of this person who is known as (your name). See this person (you) interacting with the people and other beings in his/her life. See this person moving through the motions of their life, in the places they frequent, in their home and work. What do you observe? Notice the exchanges of energy that take place. What is happening? What is the metaphor of this person's life? What do they add to those people and places around them? What recommendation would you give this person about how to be cherished, treasured and appreciated in their life?

Part B: Now let's go a step deeper. What is your connection to Spirit? If you could see that connection, what does it look like? Is there a color or shape? Is there a feeling or sound? Focus on the point between your eyebrows and furrow your brow. Is there a color?

Being from and therefore a part of Spirit, you are of inherent value to this creation. There is no one who is, and there never again will be, an exact replica of you. You are a unique creation, and therefore are of great value.

Diamond Point Directions

Part A:
- Allow yourself to be comfortable sitting or lying and become aware of your body and breath.
- Imagine yourself sitting in a theater, watching a movie of your life.
- Watch the scenes of your everyday life as a detached observer.
- What do you notice? What do you see? Hear? Feel?
- Notice the exchange of energy between people, places, animals and things.
- What is the metaphor of this life? If this were a fairy tale or child's story, what character would this person be?
- What recommendations would you give to help this person?

Part B:
- Imagine you could see this person's connection to Spirit.
- What is it like? Color? Shape? Location? Feeling? Sound?

CHAPTER 17

Respect of Self and Other

*True humility is intelligent self-respect that keeps us
from thinking too highly or too meanly of ourselves."*
— Ralph W. Sockman

Respect is defined as a feeling or understanding that someone or something is important or serious and should be treated in an appropriate manner. Value leads to respect. Respect is when there is a regard for the other, a sense of consideration, where the other is held with esteem and honor. It is equally important to hold oneself – one's Self – in the same regard. With the same amount of respect. This is when people can meet and know each other. They can work together and know that each is participating, and that each is a significant and important part of the whole. When this alchemy takes place, there is a magic that transpires. When each person respects the other and themselves in the same way, they are on equal ground, and much more can transpire between them. The result of collaboration between individuals who possess self-respect and respect for the other are amazing to behold. Not only successful collaborations, but unique and extraordinary. Some of the most important feats of science, art, music and engineering, to name a few, have been accomplished in this way. The opposite is true when there is a lack of either kind of respect.

When a person sees himself as being of greater value than another, there is a wall around them. They cannot accept help or ideas from others. They have to be right, and this creates a wall around them that is often impenetrable. They often have difficulty learning, as their need to know gets in the way of being taught. It is a sad and lonely world for the person who believes they are the only one deserving of respect.

Self-respect is often harder to come by. Not the kind of narcissistic behavior displayed by some. Not like the person that thinks they are better than others. Self-respect is when one holds oneself in equal regard with others. Not greater than, not less than. Equal.

Without self-respect, there is an energy or thought pattern that gets in the way – that prevents a true joining of the minds, and of the hearts. The lack of self-respect prevents one from being able to truly show up in any situation. There will always be one's insecurity getting in the way and preventing the uniqueness of the individual to arise. This self-respect is an inner feeling and belief that may have to be nurtured. Often, people have been treated in such a way since childhood, so that they feel they don't really matter and that their thoughts and ideas are of no worth. This is a learned belief and can be countered.

Many abuse victims suffer with feelings of low self-esteem and a feeling of being less than other people. The energy emanating from this thought pattern can lead to being used in many ways. Being used by others as scapegoats. Being used by others to do whatever seems to need doing. It can lead to the workaholic syndrome as the victim strives for worth by over-giving through work. Some are Moms who give all their energy to their family and insist on being everything for everyone in their family. Some are martyrs who throw themselves on the fire of whatever cause seems worthy. Worthier than their own health and well-being. This consciousness of a lack of respect for one's self is very destructive and can lead to serious disease.

The ability to have respect for one's self models this behavior for others and is not exclusive of caring for others. There is a good kind of selfishness that promotes health and caring for others. When others know that a person will take care of themselves, they are more honest and willing to ask for help or advice. They know that the person with self-respect will have boundaries and be able to honestly say "yes" when they can and want to help – and say "no" if they cannot help or the cause doesn't suit them. Everyone would be more willing to ask for help if they knew they weren't going to unwittingly be a burden to someone else. When we are honest about what we can and can't do, or what we want or don't want to do, this is a sign of self-respect. It encourages the same from others. There is nothing abusive or manipulative in this way of being.

The self-care that emerges from self-respect is a beacon in the world. Self-care insures that the needs of the individual are met – for who can truly know what the needs of another are? When there is self-respect, a person can ask for what they need. Some people get upset when someone in their world hasn't anticipated their need. Perhaps it is a spouse, a lover, a child, or a boss or co-worker. Instead of suffering in silence, or becoming passive-aggressive, the person could show mutual respect and talk about what their needs are. Of course, there is always a place and time for this discussion. Having it will relieve much tension and anxiety for everyone involved. There's no guesswork – and there's a much greater chance of satisfying the need or desire!

EXERCISE

Assessment of Self-Respect and Respect of Others

This is a brief exercise to allow you to ponder where you are with self-respect and respect of others. Allow yourself to be totally honest and forthcoming. No judgment or comparison. We are who we are because of how we came into the world and what experiences we have had; what we learned from our primary caregivers and the world we grew up in.

Make yourself comfortable, either sitting or lying down. Begin by breathing deeply and becoming aware of your body. This is always a good place to start. It brings us to the now.

Begin by remembering a recent time when you had to work with someone else on some type of project at work or at home. What happens for you when you work with others? Is it the same if they are family members or if they are people you don't really know? In other words, do you behave differently when you are close to someone, compared to how you behave with people who are new to you? What do you say to yourself about the other person? What do you say in your mind about yourself? Do you always have the answers? Do you need to be told what to do for fear of doing something wrong? Do you have to do things your way? Do you get frustrated with the other person or with the way they are treating you? Do you say anything? Do you always say "yes" when you want to say "no"?

These few questions will begin to give you a clue as to whether you think highly of yourself or the opposite. Of course, it is best to follow an expert when one is less experienced with some project or venture. And it's also best to take the lead if you are more experienced at something. Are you willing to do either, depending on the situation?

Remember that equality in the thought of self and other is the goal, as this equality can foster creativity in the interchanges between people. Mutual respect and admiration for all! The answers will tell you if you have low self-respect (which can be low self-esteem) or if you tend to think highly of yourself. There is room for interpretation with each specific person and in each case. What comes up for you with these questions? Where do you fall on the scale of self-respect? On the scale of respect for others?

These examples are meant to begin a dialogue with yourself about this topic. They are not a definitive resource on the topic.

Diamond Point Directions

- ◆ Sit/lie comfortably, breath deeply and notice your body.
- ◆ Recall an event of working with someone at home or at work.
- ◆ What happens inside yourself when you work with others?
- ◆ What occurs between you and the other, and with the project?
- ◆ Do you behave differently with family/friends and new people?
- ◆ What do you say inside yourself about the other person?
- ◆ What do you say inside yourself about yourself?
- ◆ Do you always have the answers?
- ◆ Do you need to be told what to do for fear of doing something wrong?
- ◆ Do you have to do things your way?
- ◆ Do you get frustrated with the way others treat you?
- ◆ Do you speak up when you are feeling unappreciated?
- ◆ Do you say "yes" when you mean "no"?
- ◆ Are you willing to take directions from a more experienced person?
- ◆ Are you willing to take the lead when you are the most experienced person?

CHAPTER 18

The Vital Exchange

*"Love cures people – both the ones
who give it and the ones who receive it."*
— Karl A. Menninger

The ability or inability to give and receive is crucial to the advent of health or disease in the body. The type of disease, the organ affected, the when and how of disease, is affected by this aspect of life.

We have several types of nourishment to sustain the body. Of course there is the food we eat and water we drink. Our bodies have to be able to take in these substances and to digest them, and then to receive the nutrition from the food. There are many steps to this process and there can be many disruptions to this normal cycle. There are those who can't take in food for various reasons, or who refuse to take in food. There are those who eat well and then cannot digest or absorb the nutrition. The exact mechanism of what is happening physically, mentally and emotionally must be verified to restore health.

There is another aspect that is vital to life: the ability to give and receive love. This most basic of needs is necessary to thrive. The heart cries for the love that it wants. It needs to grow so it can love. Life in the world of trees and other plants needs water and sunshine to live and grow. Likewise, the heart, too, needs love. Love is both the water and the sunlight. The life force is the light. The blood is the heart's water. They both nurture and are moved by the heart. The heart must have love to live and to thrive. To thrive is so much more than to just live. To thrive is to be growing and living to the fullest potential. To thrive. Imagine it. Are you ready to grow and thrive in the love that Spirit, the Universal Intelligence, is showering on you? You are loved. Spirit is sustaining you. Spirit is nourishing you in the loving bath of light.

We symbolically receive love through the food and water we consume. This we receive from the Source. The most subtle form of nutrition we must receive from the Source is the Life Force that sustains the body. This is the ultimate connection with Source that we usually don't recognize and acknowledge. This Source of Life Force is the reason we can even move, think, or eat and drink.

This life is a chance to give love and receive love. To be love itself. Where in the body do we truly live? Is it in the heart? Is your head in the way? It might be. I can now feel that my heart is tired. It needs to rest. It has been so hurt and used so badly in the past. It needs to live now. To live without worry. Without crying. Without holding on to the tears.

EXERCISE

The Heart Scan

This is an exercise to assess the state of your heart. To check in with the heart about the life it is living within you. This will allow you to know the heart's joy and worry. Whether it is receiving the love it needs and giving the love it wants to share. Discover for yourself if there is some hurt from the past that the heart is still crying over. Allow yourself to add or subtract from the suggested questions to better suit your curiosity and need.

Let your knowing of the responses appear in your mind, and take note. This is not to be figured out: simply allow it to be revealed. The heart will speak in that intuitive voice that is brief and concise. If you try too hard, you will block the inner voice. Just let go and breathe. Come back to it at another time if you need to. Sometimes, just asking the questions opens the dialogue, and the answers come later. Unlike the way many of us live our lives, pushing does not work here!

Extended Directions

Take a moment now and sit or lie down on your back. Breathe deeply several times. Tense your body with an inhale and release all tension with an exhale. Allow yourself to tune into your heart. Feel how it feels to you in this moment. Take note of all physical sensations. Does there seem to be any shape or color? Speak to your heart. Ask it how it is? Is it happy with your life? Is the heart receiving all the love it needs? Can it give the love it wants to share with the world? Is there any pain or complaint it wants you to know about? Does it need to heal in any way or from anything? Is there anything you can do or change, that would help you fully embody your heart energy?

If your heart could speak to you right now, what does it want you to know? Allow yourself to become aware of any and all messages for you. When this exchange feels complete, thank your heart for sharing with you. If you'd like to receive more timely wisdom from your heart, how can it get your attention?

Diamond Point Directions

◆ Sit or lie in a comfortable place. Breathe deeply several times.

◆ Tense all your body muscles with inhale; then exhale and release. Repeat three times.

◆ Tune in to your heart. What is the present physical sensation?

◆ Is there a shape or color? Any sound, taste or smell?

◆ Send a message to your heart. How does it respond?

◆ Ask: Is it happy? Is it receiving all the love it wants and needs?

◆ Can your heart share its love with the world?

◆ Is there any type of pain or complaint it wants you to know?

◆ Does it need any type of healing? What can you do to help?

◆ Is there anything it wants you to do or change that would help the heart energy express?

◆ What does your heart want you to know now?

◆ Ask any questions you would like. Open questions are usually better than "yes" or "no" questions.

◆ If your heart wants your attention in the future, how will it let you know? You can ask it to find out.

◆ When you have finished, thank your heart for sharing with you.

Through the Rubenfeld Synergy Training, I came to see my heart as a wonderland, not the wasteland that it had been. There was a sense of freedom in the heart. I felt as though my heart had been held too tightly, and then squished for so long that it had not been able to move for a long time. Stuck somewhere. The heart is the home. The home to Spirit, to God and Gurus. Home to the Red Cloud, the Soul.

One of my favorite spiritual chants written by Paramahansa Yogananda, my Guru, is "The Divine Gypsy." In this chant there is a reference to "The Red Cloud." The chant mentions singing to "my Red Cloud." For years I wondered what that was. What did it mean? Finally it dawned on me, as I was writing this book, that the Red Cloud was the Soul – my Soul, that I could sing to and become one with.

There is a sense of freedom that lives in the heart. The sense of freedom of the Soul. The home of the Red Cloud. The home of the Spirit is in your heart. This is where Spirit has Life. For many years, my heart had become a wasteland. Not a wonderland. The heart should be a wonderland of Love. A wonderland of love for all to feel and enjoy.

As Spirit looks out of your eyes right now, looking at your life, what does it see? What expression of Life Force is evident in your life? Holding old trauma can create an existence without life, without love, without a hope for life. Hopelessness can translate into a lack of heart. Without heart, can one live? How can one keep living without heart? Impossible in the literal sense. But, how many are walking through life without heart? Without purpose? What is your purpose now? What do you need to revivify, to renew, to re-enliven yourself, and then others?

Right now, for some, there may be sadness in the heart. The sadness over loss of life. The lost time without life. The lifelessness. There may be sadness over the loss of someone in your life. Sadness over how they lived their life. Where is the way out of these feelings? How can you live differently? How to breathe new life into yourself and those you love? How can you find the steps back into a life full of love and gusto, expressing all of your potential and uniqueness?

For some, there may be a joy and lightness that lives naturally in the heart. How might that be increased and shared with others? By shining the light of your love in the world, others will become inspired and want to shine their light also. Living the love is wonderfully attractive and enlivening to all who witness it.

EXERCISE

Find the Heart in Your Life

This exercise is an ongoing experience of your life. Start to become aware of your reactions and responses to your life. The people and experiences in your life. What makes you laugh? What makes you cry? The movie scenes, the silly commercials, something someone says or does? How do you feel when you receive or don't receive some message or present or expected package? How do you respond to those feelings? Begin to become aware of yourself and your surroundings in all situations. Get to know you. Who are you? How are you? Allow yourself to know yourself from an unattached point of view. It's okay to be just who you are. If you don't like something, you can change things. Awareness is the first step.

Diamond Point Directions

- ◆ Allow yourself to become an observer of your everyday life. Slow down a bit and take notice.
- ◆ What makes you laugh? What makes you smile?
- ◆ What makes you tear up? What makes you want to cry?
- ◆ What is it that inspires you?
- ◆ Who do you want to be around and why?
- ◆ What makes you say "Aww!" and why?
- ◆ What makes your heart sing?
- ◆ What makes you feel comfortable and comforted?
- ◆ What do you want to know about yourself?

CHAPTER 19

The Duty to Live Your Life

"The sacred duty of being an individual
is to gradually learn to live so as
to awaken the eternal within you."
— John O'Donahue

The following vision came to me during a bodywork session: First I saw myself as a little girl with my short hair. Then I saw myself as a victim of leprosy. My nose was gone, and one ear; my face was barely recognizable. Then it came to me: I can only choose me. This is the only choice. When I don't choose me, I am eaten away at: barely recognizable to myself or others. Indistinguishable as an individual with a unique heart and soul.

I remember realizing this so clearly, in Puerto Rico, when it was time to divorce. My husband was out surfing with my best friend and I was on the beach. I was boiling inside over the fights my husband and I had been having. His stupid antics were driving me mad, literally! I was wondering what I was going to do. Feeling stuck. The promise of marriage, "till death do us part. In sickness and in health." Besides, what would he do without me?

He could barely keep it together with me. At least, my version of what it was to "keep it together." What would he ever do without me? And then it hit me: "Him or me, him or me…." The words rang in my head like a bell. Over and over. "If I choose him, I will die. I must choose me." And I did. I promised myself that I would choose me. That I would choose life – over dying by living for someone else. Someone who I didn't see as loving me or even caring for my general well being. "I choose me!" Then I saw the sign from God. A lone dolphin caught the next wave and expertly surfed it right in front of me. I knew this was the right choice.

These revelations had come to me unheeded. My body was revealing the secrets it held in its tissues. In my tissues, the only choice before me again was to choose me. How could I choose the other people, the clients, the dogs, Dad or anyone else? Just like on that beach in Puerto Rico, the only choice for life was the choice for me. "I choose me" rang through my every cell. I remembered the dolphin.

As this choice for Self vibrated through my being, it evolved to "I have the right to choose me." It is the birthright I earned when I was born. It is my life, and I have the right to live it. The right to choose me in every way imaginable. To choose me in all the decisions in my life. This is my life, after all!

Then I realized that it is my duty to choose me. I have been given this life: it is a gift, and I have a duty to choose me. To live the life I was born to live. It is up to me to live to my fullest potential. Who said, "Our life is God's gift to us, and what we do with it is our gift to God?" Each of us must discover this right, this duty within ourselves. To choose ourselves. To live to our potential. To awaken the eternal within, as John O'Donahue said.

I realize that my greatest potential, my greatest goal, is to know God. I need to do whatever possible to be able to know God. To realize myself, my Soul, as being one with God. This realization of my higher purpose for being on this planet frees me to do what I need to do. Whatever I need to do to realize this higher potential and purpose. This will free me and others. For if I am doing what I need to do, others can be inspired to do what they need to do to realize their potential. This is it. The key to recovery.

This is what my overeating is all about. When I don't choose me, when I don't make decisions in line with my higher potential, then I stuff myself to push down the hurt. I feel those feelings that I'm not worth it. Not worth choosing myself over the other people, or the things that need doing. Those feelings that I don't have the right to choose me, that I'm not worth it to myself. That the others – the schedule – anything is more important than me. These are the feelings that lead to my overeating. This is what makes me ask myself, "What do I get?" and then choose some cake or sweet thing to eat.

When I allow myself to choose me, I am in control of my life. The guide to making correct choices is to always choose me. When I choose me, I choose self-worth and equality. I am of value and I am the first person to consider when making choices and decisions. This is not selfishness. This is seeing myself and others as of equal value. We both have the right to live a full life. By living a full life myself, I allow others to do the same.

Listening to the inner child allows me to hear my inner voice. What she needs or feels are my own deepest needs and feelings. Following her/me in the moment – rather than using will power and enthusiasm that fade when things don't go well, when I fail to listen to my needs. Surrendering in the moment to my right to choose me – my duty to choose me – is the pivotal point, rather than making rules to follow that will always have exceptions.

We each have our own life experience. They are supposed to be different life experiences. We each have a right. To each his own. To live our unique life experience. I have a right to live my life. I have a duty to live my life as it was meant to be for me. Not someone else's ideas. Not some one else's right. Not someone else's duty. Mine for me and for them, theirs. Now there is the equality. There are the equal rights. What an enlightened doctrine! So now comes the duty to interact with others as equals with the same rights. The duty to live this personal expression of God to the fullest. To embody and embrace that fully. I am that. God has become myself. There is the equality and respect. Since each of us is a unique expression of Spirit, each of us is the only one who can live our own unique life. Respect for ourselves and others, to live as we see fit. Not pushing our wishes on the other, nor accepting responsibility to do as others want.

EXERCISE

Living Your Unique Life

This exercise is meant to allow you the space to imagine honoring yourself. Honoring in such a way that you allow yourself to live your unique expression fully. Feeling and seeing what life would be like to trust others and yourself enough to speak and live your truth. What does that mean to you?

As you find yourself with the time and space to explore your life, be sure to breathe. Become aware of your body in the now. Appreciate that which you are noticing within yourself. Notice your physical nature, and then look deeper, into your heart. Breathe, and feel the breath move through your body. Feel your connection with your life.

Diamond Point Directions

◆ What would your life be like if you lived as if it were your duty to be your unique self?
◆ What would you do differently?
◆ What kind of work would you do?
◆ What kind of relationships would you build?
◆ What would it be like to honor yourself fully?
◆ Would there be any difference in the choices you make?

EXERCISE

Reframing Wound as Gift

This exercise is meant to allow you to reframe any messages you have given yourself about some wound you suffered at the hands of another, or that happened to you due to life's circumstances. This will allow you to cherish what you have become through that wound, and how that wound and the changes in you have brought some gift to the world. Some gift that would not have been possible if you had not lived through the experience.

Find yourself in a place that is comfortable, where you will not be disturbed. Begin with coming into the moment by breathing into your body and becoming aware of any sensations you might be experiencing. Look over your life. Is there some situation or experience that had a profound impression on you? Something that changed your way of being in the world, no matter how long ago it was? Start with what happened, then look at how it affected you and how you responded. In as few words as possible, what was the wound? What effect did this event or situation have on your psyche? Has this wound led you to work in a certain field, or has it caused you to pursue some specific dream or take up some cause? Has this experience led to your developing a certain skill? For example: reading people and their intentions, or knowing what is happening around you, though it remains unspoken?

Allow yourself to reflect and recognize your motivations. Allow yourself to realize how any injury may have led you on a journey in life that brought you to serving humanity in a specific way. Allow yourself to realize what makes you unique.

Diamond Point Directions

◆ Find a comfortable place and position and become aware of your body. Breathe.

◆ Allow yourself to see your life from a distance. Become the observer.

◆ Identify any situation or experience that had a profound effect on you.

◆ Review what actually happened.

◆ How did the event(s) affect you? How did you respond? What changed in you?

◆ Briefly state what the wound is.

◆ What was the long-term effect on your psyche? Your way of moving in the world?

◆ What field of work are you in; where and how do you live that was affected by this event?

◆ Do you have some specific cause, dream or pursuit that was seeded by this event?

◆ What skill have you developed that was directly linked to this event or experience?

◆ Has your journey in life been affected by this event?

◆ What has been a positive outcome (for yourself and for others)?

◆ What makes you the unique person that you have become?

CHAPTER 20

Judgment and Betrayal

"….judgment is never just."
— D.H. LAWRENCE

"Betrayal can only happen if you love."
— JOHN LE CARRE

I realize that I am still working on the same issues. I discovered them long ago by acting them out in my chiropractic practice in Puerto Rico. Wanting to sacrifice myself for others. Those same feelings of being unworthy that had plagued me then – the feelings that my only worth was what I could do for others. The pain that I might take into and onto myself to justify my existence.

My betrayal of myself, by judging and not valuing myself, continues to plague my deepest subconscious streams of thought. I have been finding and unearthing the roots of this, and their relationship to present-day life. Great discovery! This is how I get myself to feel betrayed by others in my life. It actually comes from within me! Had it come from the betrayal early in life?

From the abusers? They betrayed me at that early, formative age, and therefore it had become a part of my psyche? I have seen betrayal everywhere outside myself. I had felt betrayed by my parents when they chose to move from Puerto Rico. They moved after I had returned there post-college to open my first chiropractic practice. I had felt betrayed by both of my husbands. Different friends over the years have done things that left me feeling betrayed. It was as if, once people get close to me, they might become part of the "Betray Toni Club." Had I taken in that early betrayal by the abusers, and made it into a way of connecting through disconnection with others? Such a puzzle, and yet, there is some truth to this vantage point. And then, there is always the deeper issue of betraying myself by overworking, overeating and overspending that I have fallen into.

Finally discovering the deeper theme makes me sick and tired and scared! How does one ever emerge from the death grip of this theme? Once again to pick myself up and start over. Little by little with treating the body in a kind and thoughtful way. Better food, and less "bad" food. More movement. More passion for life and what it has to offer. Following the sparks of life shown to me by the reaction of enthusiasm. What do I like? What and who make my heart sing? What moves my heart to vibrate with life? Vibrate with love for the world – remembering always that the motivation needs to be genuine and coming from within. Listening to the inner voice of heart from the inner child. Not the plans of the educated mind that knows the rules and how to use will power to force her way. The rules can only last so long. There must be a moment-to-moment choosing of life and love over self-betrayal and a slow death.

EXERCISE

Counteracting Personal Judgment

Do you judge yourself in any way? Your body, your voice, your achievements? Are there things or ways of being that you observe in yourself that you are judging as wrong or unworthy? Do you label yourself in any judgmental ways? Do you call yourself names, or belittle or berate yourself?

Allow yourself to notice how you talk to yourself in your head. Are you nice, and supportive? Do you forgive your mistakes? Do you have any phrases to encourage yourself? Do you like yourself?

This exercise is meant to support your exploration of exchanging judgment for encouragement. It may be something that you need to work on over time. Start where you are with this, and look for ways to increase the amount of support and love that you can convey to yourself. Only increase this in relation to how much you can tolerate. Many people have trouble with this. Being truly nice to ourselves in our own self-talk is not something our society encourages. Many times we are "good" to ourselves by eating, drinking, imbibing things that are actually harmful to us. Think about it. How do you give a "treat" to yourself?

Detailed Directions

Find a place to relax, and begin with some deep breathing. Allow yourself to become aware of any places holding tension in your body or your breath. These places will tighten with difficult moments, and release with breakthrough moments. Speak to yourself in a supportive and loving way. What might you say that you would perceive as loving and supportive? If you can't think of anything, imagine that you are speaking to a child you love, or a pet. What would you say to show encouragement and love to them? Try saying those things to yourself. What response does your body have? What is it like for you to give this loving support to you? If it is difficult, notice this. Is there a way to encourage yourself that you can accept? Try to be as encouraging and as loving as is possible for you, and see what happens in your body.

Diamond Point Directions

◆ Allow yourself to sit or lie in a comfortable place, and breathe.

◆ Become aware of your body and any places of tension. Use them to detect breakthroughs or "tough spots."

◆ Speak to yourself in a loving and supportive way. What is your body's response?

◆ If this is difficult, imagine how you would encourage a child or a beloved pet. Use those words.

◆ Take note of how much love and encouragement you can accept from yourself without judgment.

◆ Work on this for brief periods, as tolerable. Write or draw your expression of this experience.

There are many ways that we may be betrayed by others or by circumstances in this life. We must look at our wounds. Sometimes a physical wound hurts so badly that we don't want anyone to look at it, for fear of hurting it worse. Just like those physical wounds that need to be seen to be tended to, these wounds of betrayal must be exposed to the light of day, to the light of Spirit, so that we can begin to heal them.

EXERCISE

Healing Wounds of Betrayal

Detailed Directions

Betrayal is one of the deepest wounds. It is not to be trivialized. Carrying it with you can continue to cause you injury. We will look here at a way to work with betrayal, to lessen its sting, and to see it from a different perspective. Seek professional assistance if you know you have the tendency to have extreme reactions to the material you are about to broach, or if you have a hard time returning to your normal life after thinking about this topic.

Allow yourself to lie in a comfortable place, and be sure you are safe and warm. The most privacy possible would be wonderful, and knowing that loving support is available, should you need it, is also an advantage. Wrap yourself in a blanket and have water or hot tea and whatever else makes you feel comforted close by. Lie with your knees bent up and your feet firmly on the floor. This will help to ground you. Breathe as if you have nostrils on the bottom of your feet: up your legs, from your feet, and continuing up into the body. Breathe out from the lungs to the bottoms of your feet. Continue with this for several minutes, bringing in calmness and the sense of being grounded.

Recall only one instance of being betrayed. If you can't identify one – congratulations! You might not have ever been betrayed. It is possible there is something buried deep in your psyche, and if it is not emerging readily it probably is better left where it is.

If you have identified an instance of being betrayed, allow yourself to experience it in your body. Where do you feel it in your body? What does it feel like physically? Keep breathing into and out of your feet. Allow yourself to forgive yourself for this having happened. You did nothing wrong. Stay with this until you can believe that you are innocent in the betrayal. No matter what you may have done or not done, there is no excuse for betrayal. Notice if there has been any change in the way you are experiencing your body. Continue to breathe in and out of your feet. What have you learned about life from this experience? Can you take that learning in, and appreciate that it has value for you? Stay with this until you have found any value that you can recognize.

If there is any anger at the person or circumstance, allow yourself to see the responsible person in your mind's eye. Express the anger, hurt, disappointment, hatred (whatever comes up for you) to that person. The best is to actually express yourself out loud. This is very powerful in allowing your system to release the pain and process the memory in another way. A step removed is to see yourself talking, yelling, screaming, or whatever is necessary to express to that person how you feel. Notice any changes in the way you experience your body now.

The most important part of this experience is to allow yourself to fully express what never was expressed to the person who betrayed you. You may want to see in your mind's eye how they respond, and if they have anything to express to you. Having a "conversation," if you will. It is a little tricky carrying on this conversation on your own, and this may best be reserved for when you are with a professional. Knowing when to stop this process is just as important as doing it!

Remember, the most important part is allowing yourself to express fully to the betrayer – saying everything there is to say now, with the emotion that is charged with the memory.

Diamond Point Directions

- ◆ Lie on your back, in a safe, comfortable, private place.
- ◆ Have things that comfort you close by.
- ◆ Bend your knees up and breathe into your feet.
- ◆ Bring calmness and grounding into your body.
- ◆ Recall only one instance of feeling betrayed. Where is the memory in your physical body?
- ◆ What does it feel like in this place? Any colors, shapes, sounds, smells or tastes?
- ◆ Keep breathing in and out of your feet.
- ◆ Forgive yourself. You did nothing wrong.
- ◆ If self-forgiveness impossible, stay with the breath.
- ◆ Once you are calm again, notice any physical changes.
- ◆ What have you learned about life from this experience?
- ◆ Counter negatives by finding the value in your life now.
- ◆ Hold anyone you have anger for in your mind's eye.
- ◆ Express your feelings to this person(s) out loud.
- ◆ If this is too difficult, see yourself sitting in a theater, watching yourself on a stage in front of you.
- ◆ Watch yourself expressing to this person(s).
- ◆ Notice what is happening in your body now.
- ◆ Become aware of breath and your feet on the floor.
- ◆ Let the exercise go, sit up gently, drink water, get up and walk around with purpose, feeling the ground.

CHAPTER 21

Conversation with the Inner Child

"Caring for your inner child has a powerful
and surprisingly quick result:
Do it and the child heals."
— Martha Beck

The following is the result of working with myself as suggested in the exercise below.

After breathing deeply for several minutes, I scan for physical sensations:

The chest feels and looks like a small metal compact. Something like what my mother would put her blush in.

I realize: The little girl is in there. My little one... me.

Adult: Have you gone hiding again?

Little girl: Yes. You are not listening to me. You are coming to your own conclusions.

A: What is it like to be frozen?

LG: It is cold and dark and lonely.

A: Where do you go?

LG: I get very still. That is why you are slow now. You don't like me.

A: Yes I do. I love you.

LG: No you don't. You want me to go away so you can be fast and have fun without me.

A: I can never have fun without you!

LG: You lie!

A: I haven't known for very long that you were there.

LG: Really?

A: Just recently I realized you were there. Lauren helped me find you.

(Silence)

A: I want to write more, but I want to listen to you, too. Do you want to write some more?

LG: I guess.

A: What do you want to write about?

LG: Animals.

A: What kind of animals?

LG: There are two kinds. Good ones and bad ones.

A: What are the good ones?

LG: Like dogs and cats and horses.

A: And what are the bad ones?

LG: People that hurt you.

A: The people that hurt you are like animals?

LG: Animals that are mean and bite and make grunting sounds and they just want to eat and eat.

They ate me up.

A: If they ate you up, how are you here now?

LG: I hid, inside you, inside your chest.

A: Anything else you want to say about animals?

LG: The bad ones don't have a heart. Their heart is hurt, that is why they hurt me.

That is why they hurt people.

A: What can we do?

LG: They need help, but they are scary.

A: Do you mean that I should help them?

LG: Yes, maybe this book can help them. Help them see what they do to people when they hurt them.

A: Maybe. You would have to help me a lot. I don't know about these animals.

LG: Yes you do…

A: Maybe I do.

LG: Yes, you have known men that are like animals. Men that prey on many animals. The ones who eat and eat and then don't know when to stop. They eat other animal-like people up.

A: You mean they feed on the fear, the sex, what else?

LG: Their insecurity. The man knows they want the animal energy he has, so he gives it to them. They want him to eat them.

A: You'll have to say more.

LG: It is the energy. The energy that the wounded put out. It is in their field. The field of their aura, their energy. The field emanates from them. It is in their tone of voice, the words they use, the look in their eye. He knows. He knows. He senses it like the animal he is.

A: What to do about it?

LG: The wounded need to become aware of the energy they are emanating from their core. The grooves in their brain, their thoughts, put that energy into all they are. Their walk, their talk, their energy, their look, everything.

A: What can I do about that?

LG: You have to find a way to teach them. To help them see, feel, know.

A: But I can't even get myself to feel sometimes! I can't feel you!

LG: Yes you can. I am in that spot in your chest, but I could be bigger. I could grow up and help you see who you are.

A: Yes! Please grow up and let me see who you are! I need to know who you are so I can grow up and grow into who I can be. I'll never be able to help anyone else if I don't have you inside me to guide me. You are the one who knows, who sees. Can you please wake up and come out and let me know who you are? I am dying to know you. I am dying without you. My heart that was sucked dry cannot survive another minute without having you come back. Come back and live in your place. The place where you get very still is your throne. Not your cage. Can you, will you, come live on your throne? Don't hide! Please don't hide! Please come out!

LG: You don't want me.

(Silence)

A: I really want to include you. It means that I have to slow down, doesn't it!?

LG: At least slow enough to feel. Once you can feel me you can speed back up.

It is not about being fast, but being in tune.

A: I understand what you are intimating about the "animals". I'm not sure I can help them. Not sure what my role is. Not sure if I can do anything unless I'm not scared of them. They want to eat you up. They might hurt us again. They might make us fall.

LG: The animal: he doesn't think he has value either. He learned from the one who gave him the attention he needed. He learned to do sexual things to make them happy. He learned the energy of the insatiable desire for sexual satisfaction. That which is never satisfied. He strives to fulfill that. He now has it, and he cannot be satisfied. He looks for the energy he had as a child, that got taken away from him, and he wants to devour that from others. He needs it.

Guru: **You are loved!** (I hear the Guru's voice in my head.)

LG: This is what I've been longing for all my life. What I've been unable to believe. Unable to accept. I feel my heart full of Guru's Love. I see his face smiling and feel his closeness in my heart and in my third eye.

A: There it is, the twinge of the third eye. Is it opening or twitching? I am not sure.

(Silence)

A: The place in my chest is very still. This is always the center of the sadness. The center of the pain. This is the fear, and the young me is there. This is where she lives. She lives in there. It feels still and somewhat hard. This is the little one. I will now write from there. I have my eyes closed, and I will go in there. I am afraid to go in there. I am afraid there. There are many tears here. This is the place that holds back. This is the place that I don't let anyone in. Even me! It is about the size of a softball in diameter now. I am distracted. Go back there.

Words come: What is wrong with you! The meanness is there. The being mean to myself. What is wrong with you? Why can't you do what they want without crying? What is wrong with you? Stay with it.

I am so mad at you for feeling. What is it about you that always feels the pain? Why can't you not feel the pain? Why do you hold onto the pain?

LG: It is the only thing I have. The pain is the only thing that I can feel.

A: Don't stop. Stay with it. It feels hard like a softball, too. It does go deep into my chest. It goes into my chest. It is a hole that has been covered up. The hole that was left inside when he left me there, hurt. Why did he leave me there, hurt? I was bad. Why did Mom leave me there, hurt? It was my fault. Let the tears come now. It is okay. You don't need to hide from me any more. Let it come; now is the time.

LG: What are softballs for?

A: They are for hitting. Hitting with a bat.

LG: For throwing, throwing away my life. That is what they did to me. They wanted to throw me away. They did throw me away. Like trash. Like a softball...

A: Breathe into that place. Stay with it, Toni! She is the one who never got heard. She is the one who has been stuck in there for all these years.

Tell me your name.

LG: Toni.

A: Where are you from, little one?

LG: My mommy.

A: What is the matter?

LG: I'm scared.

A: What are you scared of?

LG: Scared you're going to leave me, leave me there, leave me alone! (Tears...)

(We got up and we stretched. It was so intense! I had to move.

Here we go. Can I contact that place at this pace again?)

A: Now it is not a softball. It feels empty. Are you there?

LG: Uh huh.

A: What are you doing?

LG: Hiding.

A: Can you talk to me now?

LG: I don't know.

A: Lets try.

LG: Okay.

A: What is your color?

LG: Yellow.

A: Do you like that?

LG: Yes.

A: Tell me how you feel.

LG: I'm frozen.

A: Frozen?

LG: Yes.

A: I'm thinking that you are in shock.

LG: Maybe. I don't know what that means.

A: How scared are you?

LG: I have no feeling, I'm frozen.

A: What emotions do you have?

LG: Scared, dead, then some stirring. Am I waking up?

A: What if you did?

LG: I'm not sure what would happen. Can I?

A: Yes you can wake up. I won't stuff you down again.

LG: Yes you will. You've been stuffing me down for years!

A: I don't know how to move when you are up, when you are awake.

LG: Then how can I wake up?

A: When you said we would slow down to go in another direction, is this it?

LG: Yes. This place is slow and very hard to keep open

A: It feels like there is sticky stuff in there. Did someone else abuse you too?

What stories do you hold, little girl?

LG: I'm not telling.

A: I need you to tell me so I can help you.

LG: You are going to take me out in front of other people

A: Maybe.

LG: They might laugh, they might hurt me.

A: This is the heart of the matter. The heart is metaphorical and meaningful. (I feel a gulf in my chest.) Is there a gulf here?

LG: Yes, This is *the gulf of love that exists in the abused.*

This is the part of my chest that pressed against the couch when he pushed my head up and down. The cushions were soft but the couch edge was hard. It hurt. I couldn't get away. He held me tight. What to do? Who will help me? They brought me here. Where are they?

(Long pause, tears, breathing)

A: I am listening to you. In fact, I'm going to let you write now. Are you ready to take over writing?

LG: I think so.

A: How am I going to let you keep writing? How will I know that it is you writing and not the adult me? What are the signs and symptoms?

LG: I will write like waves and you keep your eyes closed and not editing any spelling or grammar. Okay?

Feel me in your chest. I am the hard spot. I am the soft spot. I am the one who needs you to listen. You are the one who talks and doesn't listen.

I am a tomato that is sour and sweet. I am juicy, and I can be dry and tasteless, or full of juice and taste.

You are the careful one who doesn't want the energy to move. You squeeze it down. Stop it.

I hold the reins to the feelings. I have something to teach. I am the one you need to listen to. I am your heart. I have been caged and tortured for years. Caged when your heart broke, and then kept there by years of neglect and abuse by you.

What I need now is for it to be free. I need to bleed. Do not be afraid. Feel the bleeding. This is the way to have new blood flow into the body and brain and system that has been shut off for so many years. I will lead, but you must put me first. I must be allowed to check out the scene before you decide what to do. Before you decide a course. You must wait and let me gauge the situation.

Stop, breathe, and wait for the sign. The sign that I have decided. I am the heart. I am your guide. You have kept me young, and stuck, and now I want to move. I can be grown. I can decide. I can see; I can feel.

I am slow. I don't rush. I feel my way. I meditate with pleasure. Sraddha (the heart's natural love) is my name. You will learn from me. Sraddha is your path. The path you were meant to live, to teach, to write.

Guru: Here is the message: When the little one's emotions and feelings are ignored and blocked, the adult freezes her, and she stays young and out of touch with the reality of her present life.

Breathe into her. Breathe into her, and let her fill with the breath of life. She will grow quickly.

A: She has grown into me. I am sraddha of the heart. It is the factor of love that sustains the universe. This is what fills us up.

LG: If you had but come to me first, you would not make wrong decisions. I am in tune with God and Gurus. I am the light, the energy and the way. How can you be lost if you look to me first?

Guru: I am the guru within who guides you if you will let me. There is a peace and calm within now. I am here.

LG: Breathe into me. I am ready for you. Don't be afraid to feel what I am feeling. It will inform you about your life.

A: Thank you!

EXERCISE

Conversation with Your Inner Child

We all have an inner child who could give us some insight and guidance at one time or another. The child was innocent, and often, in learning about the world, something was surprising or hurtful. Talking with this part of ourselves can resolve present-day issues or help heal hidden wounds. Not everyone suffered from childhood abuse as I did (thank goodness!), but there are many who did. Not everyone even remembers when there was abuse. Our minds are brilliant in their resilience, and/or their ability to block what would not serve us if we knew about it. Regardless, conversing with the inner child can be helpful. I emphasize "conversing with," not "talking to." Many people like to "talk to" or "at" someone else – especially their inner child or other personified parts of themselves. The idea of a conversation is that one person speaks, and then pauses to let the other respond. Some people find their inner child hiding, or unable or unwilling to speak. If that is the case, just be nice and do not force them in any way. It may take several sessions to "visit" first, and let them see you are serious, before they will interact with you. Don't give up. I know it feels strange. And it is very effective! Do you wonder what your little one has to share with you?

Directions

Prepare yourself by being in a private place where you won't be disturbed. Lie or sit comfortably and take several deep breaths. Become aware of the physical sensations of your body. Try to see yourself as a young child, with whatever image pops into your head first. Notice your age. How do you look or feel to your adult self? Either one of you can begin the conversation, and continue as you would as if talking to anyone else. Be polite and respectful, as you would in any conversation. Speak in short, non-complicated sentences, as if to a young child. You'll know it is the child talking back when the answers are short and simple. Otherwise, it is your left brain. Continue for as long as you are comfortable. If you become agitated, STOP! Consult a professional before continuing. If all goes well, you might consider asking this aspect of yourself to stay close, somewhere in your body. Be sure to thank this part of you for being willing to share.

Diamond Point Directions

- ◆ Find a safe, comfortable, private place to lie down or sit.
- ◆ Become aware of the breath and the ground.
- ◆ Notice all physical sensations.
- ◆ Ask your inner child to show him- or herself. Notice the approximate age.
- ◆ How does the little one look or feel to the adult you?
- ◆ Begin the conversation simply. "Hello, how are you?" is fine.
- ◆ Speak simply and in short sentences. Allow time for responses. Watch for physical responses.
- ◆ When done with the conversation, thank the little one.
- ◆ If you are comfortable with the idea, invite the little one to reside somewhere in your body.
- ◆ Establish a way the little one can get your attention if he/she needs or wants to.

CHAPTER 22

Give Yourself a Deep Breath

*"Self-realization is the knowing – in body, mind, and soul –
that we are one with the omnipresence of God;
that we do not have to pray that it come to us,
that we are not merely near it at all times,
but that God's omnipresence is our omnipresence;
that we are just as much a part of Him
now as we ever will be.
All we have to do is improve our knowing."*

— PARAMAHANSA YOGANANDA

We already are that which we seek. In following our dreams, in listening to our longings and our dissatisfaction, we begin to hear the cues and clues that lead to our healing. As we take a step back and observe our physical sensations, our recurring emotions, the repeating patterns in our lives, we begin to know ourselves. We can begin to understand what our life is telling us. The first step is awareness – noticing that which our senses tell us and that which our intuition allows us to receive from Soul, from Source.

The exercises in this book are a beginning and a practice. A practice that you can utilize as often as it serves you. By using them, you open doors to awareness of yourself and your life. Doors that may have been only partially open before.

You can design a practice that allows you access to the inner wisdom of your body, mind and soul. Start with the first exercise of breath, and make that a daily ritual. Get to know your breath and what it tells you about your present state. Your breath is your ally, and it will indicate your state of mind. A quick and shallow breath signals danger and distress to your body, and indicates a desperation and unsettled state of mind. By noticing this, and calming your breath, you will calm your mind. Remember that calmness is the prerequisite of intuition – the bridge between your ego's "monkey mind" and your soul's omniscience. As you calm your breath, your mind calms too, and you become centered, and able to receive guidance from Source.

From this calm place, of body and mind, you are able to be your optimal Self. From this vantage point, you can observe the details and patterns of your life. Then you can utilize what you have learned within this book to your best advantage.

Explore what the body is telling you through its language, the language of physical sensation. Discover the messages of the aches, pains and other symptoms. Through allowing yourself to feel all the sensations, you will start to be able to feel the pleasant and joyous sensations of life in your body!

Allow the recurring emotions to inform you about the lessons you are here to learn. That which is most upsetting or evocative is important! Not to be avoided, but to be observed, witnessed and investigated with interest, as a scientist would observe a subject.

You are your own most interesting subject – the project you are here to know, inside and out.

Learn about the inner workings of your body. Understand your body and mind, and you will not fear it. Many people feel betrayed or scared of their body. "What is it doing to me? To my life?" Well, it is telling you about your life and how you are living it. Trust the body. Your body knows what it is doing, and it wants you to know, too. It is not a machine to carry your head around! It is a miracle, designed to support our life here on Earth and allow us to evolve.

There are those who want to live a purely spiritual life, and ignore the body or transcend it completely. However, we are here incarnate in these bodies and we must give the body its due. Not to become overly sensitive or indulgent of it, but to honor it and care for it and allow it to inform us. As Deepak Chopra said once: "Our body is eavesdropping on our thoughts all the time." And it is responding to them in kind. It produces results that are in direct concert with our deepest thought patterns.

We may not even be aware of the thought patterns that we most habitually entertain. Oftentimes we are not even consciously aware of our deepest beliefs. By listening to our bodies, observing our daily lives and activities, our emotions and habits, we will learn what those deep, unspoken thought patterns are. That is where the deepest healing lies. When we change our thoughts, we change our lives and our bodies.

This book has served you as a primer of sorts, to offer tools. Valuable tools that will allow you to develop that intuitive sense that is inherent in each of us. Listening with our senses to ourselves, with awareness as the primary tool to allow our knowing. A knowing of ourselves, as Yogananda mentions above, in body, mind and soul as One with the omniscience of God, or creator, or source, or Goddess, or Allah, whatever term you want to use.

As you journey on this path with me, you now have the tools that will allow you to delve deeper into that knowing of Self. This life is an adventure and an excellent drama. We all have our ups and downs, struggles and triumphs. There are times when it seems we are working the same issues again and again. Many times we are. Healing is a spiral – and we revisit the same places, wounds, issues, feelings – all from different levels on the spiral. These things come around again, giving us a chance to notice how we want to respond this time. What can we learn on this turn around the proverbial mulberry bush? Are we here to experience? To learn through experience, and thereby grow and evolve? I believe so. Don't be concerned by the seeming repetition. Your noticing the similarities in situations, experiences and feelings lets you know you are progressing. You noticed, didn't you? Awareness first, then action. Perhaps a different action this time. A different direction, not to end up in the exact same place, but to move along while learning. Take heart! We are all in this together. It is our shared human drama.

Enjoy what you've learned here! Take what serves you. Utilize it to improve your knowing of your self and your life. I look forward to sharing insights as they come in the future. My best wishes on your adventurous travels through life! You can find me online at *ToniLuisaRivera.com*, or on Facebook or Twitter by the same name. Be well!

AFTERWORD

There is a need to emphasize the presence of a living intelligence within all of us that creates the body, sustains it and heals any disease. This intelligence is in every cell and in all creation. We can communicate with this wisdom through intuition. All people are intuitive, and this skill, like any other, can be developed.

My mission, in creating experiential workshops and writing future books, is twofold. First, to share with others how to contact that life force within, to understand the unique nature of their own intuition, and then how to commune with it. By strengthening the relationship with that inner knowing, each person can guide their own life, confident in making choices that are correct for them. These decisions can range from what shoes or mattress to buy to what job opportunity is best, or even to which person is best to become involved with. Without this inner compass, we are left to make decisions based solely on intellectual reasons, pro-and-con lists and the advice of outside sources. Each of us contains, at our very core, the greatest source of knowledge about ourselves and our own best choices.

The second part of my mission is to facilitate other healthcare professionals, regardless of their license and training, to use their enhanced intuitive capability with themselves to inform them in contacting that reservoir of information within another person. Then, by using the knowledge obtained, to deliver individualized, custom care to each client. This will result in a heightened expression and health of that living intelligence at the center of each person's Being, rendering quicker, more effective results.

About the Cover Art

The Heart of the Soul

From the beginning, I was honored that Toni wanted to use my art on the cover of her book. Knowing her to be one of the most respected and sought-after healers in Santa Fe, I consider it a great privilege to be one of the first to read her manuscript. I must say, never have I encountered so much honesty in someone's writing in my life. This is an important book. My humble hope is that the art somehow provides a visual impact that reflects the impact of her courage in writing this book.

My prayer is that the art shown to me will have a beneficial, healing impact on any who experience it. My teacher, Yogacharya J. Oliver Black, said about the creative process (speaking here specifically about great poets), that they *"await the inner condition where the poetry writes itself."* I try to take this idea to heart and apply it when creating my artwork.

This image came into my consciousness with a particular thrill. I have never heard a negative word about the piece; on the contrary, many relate very special experiences. For example, I am told by the owner of the art that under certain conditions at sunset, the art is surrounded by a glow. I have also been told that the image dates back to similar spiritual images from the time of Atlantis, and its re-emergence is a harbinger of positive energy moving forward – call it *The Propelled Heart*.

Surely, anyone who takes into their heart the inspiration to bravery that this book gives – the bravery needed for their own healing journey – will find their heart taking wing. Many blessings to all who do.

In friendship,
Carl Schuman

Fine art prints available online at *carlschumanstudio.com*

ABOUT THE AUTHOR

Toni Luisa Rivera, Doctor of Chiropractic, graduated from Life Chiropractic College in Marietta, Georgia in 1985. Toni interned with world-renowned chiropractor, Dr. Larry J. Trowell, in Davenport, Iowa, for her last two years of college. This prepared her for the opening of her first private practice in Aguadilla, Puerto Rico, shortly after graduation. As soon as the sign for *Clinica Quiropractica Rivera* was mounted, the office began to fill with patients. By the end of the first four months of her practice, Dr. Toni was serving seventy people a day. In Puerto Rico, her cases were anything but routine. Being in a rural part of the island, her office was the last resort for most people. There were no other options, and the reputation of the young woman who worked with only her hands started to grow. During those eight years in practice in Puerto Rico, Dr. Rivera saw cases that most chiropractors would never see during their entire career. She learned that complete healing comes through the ability to access body wisdom. The practitioner and the client are active in the healing process when this ability is developed by both.

Dr. Rivera's fascination with the body/mind/emotion/spirit connection grew, and she strove to learn more by studying and taking trainings. Upon discovering the wisdom and skill of Ilana Rubenfeld, founder of the Rubenfeld Synergy Method, she found the path she had sought: the path that led to a deep understanding of the bridge of intuition, which allows access to the wisdom of the soul.

Dr. Toni integrated the listening hand of Rubenfeld Synergy with her hands-on skill and knowledge of the anatomy and physiology of the body. She became part of the faculty for the Rubenfeld Synergy Method Training Institute, and mastered the teaching of others. Her forte is the creation of exercises that allow students to gain access to the wisdom of the soul through the bridge of intuition.

Now, after thirty years in private practice and experience with thousands of clients and students, Dr. Rivera has founded *Intuition Mastery*. Her dream of facilitating others in the development of their own intuitive skills has come to fruition.

INDEX TO EXERCISES